OUT OF BODY INTO MIND

An Ultra-Reflective Memoir

Milo Weston

authorHOUSE®

AuthorHouse™
1663 Liberty Drive
Bloomington, IN 47403
www.authorhouse.com
Phone: 833-262-8899

Published by AuthorHouse 11/20/2023

ISBN: 979-8-8230-1739-8 (sc)
ISBN: 979-8-8230-1740-4 (e)

Library of Congress Control Number: 2023921582

Print information available on the last page.

Interior Image Credit: Millie Weston

This book is printed on acid-free paper.

ACKNOWLEDGMENTS

To my Friends,

Regardless of whether our relationship flourished or faded, I'd like to extend my sincerest gratitude to you. As you know, I tend to lead a fairly solitary life, but you are special to me in many ways because I gravitated toward you and kindled our bond over the years. Please know the experiences we've shared continue to shape who I am psychologically, socially, and creatively. Thank you for challenging my tendencies, listening, and being a grand peace in my visions. Your continuous support throughout this journey has not gone unnoticed.

To my Parents,

Having witnessed your selflessness over the past score, I commend you for your sacrifices so I could have a shot in life and for the values you instilled in each of my siblings, as well. Reminiscing, it's almost unbelievable how far we've come together, and I thank God for the fruits of your labor I enjoy today.

To the Savior,

Last but certainly not least, I humbly thank You for sending Your only son, Jesus, to earth to share Your blessed word and be crucified, so that in time we, as unworthy sinners, could experience the ultimate freeing gift of everlasting life by truly believing and trusting in Your finished work on the cross. May these messages be in accordance with Your will for us.

You could be anywhere in the world doing
anything else with your precious time, but you're
spending it here, briefly, and I appreciate that.

To you, Son,
The truth.
You must be so exhausted.
You've spent over a decade attempting to escape it.
You've done everything in your power to ignore it.
You've gone to humiliating lengths to suppress it.
Ridiculously, you've even explored the ends of this
world's temporary distractions to deny it, and yet,
here you are, finally acknowledging it and putting
your past flawed ways to rest in good health.

Some may scorn you. Some may believe you're delusional. Some may question your sanity and validity, but you understand this is the most grounded you've ever been. In life, there comes a time to listen, a time to wonder, and a time to speak. You find yourself between a rock and a hard place with this one, though. Boundless is the metaphor you could deploy to drive your points across, but you carefully selected these. The dark ages have passed. The time has come to share your story and afflictions to provide a clear glimpse of the neurosis and beauty between your ears, young one. Don't you see? You needed to go to those places to arrive here. Cerebral freeness is within reach, so capture it. Don't you dare let that reflective flame die out. You know what you must do, because I've thrown you into this profound realm of possibility and loss. Here for a vapor, sure, but you now understand and accept what to offer before vanishing. Only you are capable of accepting your impairments wholeheartedly and continuing through the truth.

sighs

The truth.

—*God*

THE EPIPHANY (INTRODUCTION)

The surreal moment happened to land on frosty December 18, 2022. My mother, Theresa, and my younger sister Rose and I were returning to my university's campus following a brunch celebration for my second-eldest sister Millie, who had just completed her undergraduate studies. With our infamously mischievous dog Buster and Rose fast asleep in the back seat, I struck up a thought-provoking spiritual conversation with my mother. We exchanged several passionate lines and information nuggets, but it came time for me to spew a rare monologue. I expressed "rare" because unless I'm with a close friend, or "dawg," I'm usually a person of relatively few words. An eerie silent spell in the vehicle came about upon the conclusion of the methodical speech. Taking my eyes off the snow-laden evergreen trees momentarily, I turned and mystically asked, "So, do you think I could do it? I know God has been speaking to me subtly about using my talents for good, and I've just had this, um—uninspired, empty feeling since college started. I feel like writing a book might be the first major step in speaking out to this world, and you know as well as anyone I have things on my mind."

As my mother often does, she waited a few seconds to respond. When she did, she exclaimed, "Well, all I know is you were grumpy the whole weekend, but today you're like a completely different person." Processing this, I traced my grumpiness back to lack of sleep from an exhausting finals week and traced my tranquility back to the fact that before we left for brunch, I read the Ephesians epistle from the hotel room's Gideon Bible, underlined a handful of peace-focused verses, and placed it on our room's nightstand in hopes that the room keeper would entertain a quick glance, at least.

As we arrived near campus two hours later, we unanimously decided that Red Robin was the destination for our last meal together before Christmas. During the suspenseful minutes spent awaiting a monstrous Red's Tavern Double Burger, nothing short of an amalgamation of thoughts traveled at warp speed in my mind. I cross-referenced the abstract thoughts I've experienced mentally since high school with newfound views of the conversation-filled day and immediately noticed that all the insightful, but mysteriously distant, think pieces roaming loosely in my consciousness were beginning to fit together like mechanisms in a complex clock. To exaggerate and illustrate a touch, it felt like I had an otherworldly epiphany while scarfing down my half-pound beef burger with extra Campfire Sauce. In all seriousness, though, the events taking place that afternoon fused the development of the ultrareflective memoir your mind is fixed upon.

The seemingly never-ending time wherein the collection of visions and think pieces were loosely roaming provided me with ample moments and headspace to develop a body of work encompassing select bizarre, melancholic, and triumphant events of my past. In recent memory, I think of the lone work shifts after school, restless nights, anxiety-ridden Sundays, and eclectic college experiences involving an absurd amount of concentration in attempting to relinquish the chaotic flow of guilty feelings from thinking I was supposed to be doing something else, anywhere else, all the time. Awkward and nearly irreparable like an itch on the inner part of the shoulder blade, easing those feelings were possible temporarily, but at the expense of my physiological being and general disposition. To people without these uncommon ways, I understand any difficulty or frustration in actively sympathizing with the peculiar behavior of individuals with neurosis and the mental impairment termed "obsessive-compulsive disorder." Odd behavior is merely one aspect of the phenomena, the only applicable aspect for those without the condition. I am honored to bring forth to you other aspects, aspects unexplored by many: the inescapable thoughts and scenes those thoughts are destined to trickle into.

A trip into an unusual mind fashioned similarly to a winding road with a few stops you did not know you needed is the route to a psychological and spiritual destination so magical, it's almost inconceivable. This campaign begins in the early stages of my life and progresses steadily with four chronological phases until I reached age twenty. There are three thoughtful, challenging bridges, or as I refer to them, "mind relics," heavily inspired by and featuring content from the Book of Proverbs and Marcus

Aurelius's *Meditations* that may kindle an appreciation for facets of self-love, wisdom, and stoic thinking, even if it's facilitated by a young individual with no considerable accolades, degrees, accomplishments, or inventions. My intention is to extend a bright testament to those who feel they have nothing to mind but darkness. There are levels to our troubles, and mine will prove minuscule in the grand scheme, but the human experience demands sound words spread on every level. It took a substantial amount of internal deliberation to decide whether to expose various vulnerabilities of my past in these writings, but I realized the enlightened comprehension of this moral message, and the hope it might instill, transcends any negative criticism. This is much more important than just me, and it was high time I recognized that fact.

As I wrote earlier, a multitude of underlying factors contributed to the development of this curated mix of English, such as nostalgia, total confusion, a whirlwind of thoughts, COVID-19, depressing college semesters, immense gratitude, and the overwhelmingly warm energy and feedback from the delightful folks I'd spoken to regarding my creative ideas and visions. Without a shadow of a doubt, though, coming to know Jesus Christ as my personal savior was the most authoritative force. I'm taking firm hold of the responsibility I feel as a fortunate person to spread an anecdote-based message steeped in truth and meaning to those so inclined to read on. Know that I do not take this responsibility lightly. I simply could not, in decent conscience and heart, continue to go about my days knowing full well there are people of different ages, backgrounds, races, and religious affiliations who would have the opportunity to digest some or all of the following thoughts and memories and live a clearer, more peaceful life because of it. That established, feel free to join us today as we time travel to explore the real and the fake, the truth and the lies, the highs and the lows, and the thoughts and the screams.

[Therapy—9:30 a.m.]

"Good morning, Milo."

"Morning. I really like these chairs—solid lumbar support."

"Yes! I wish I had them in my own house."

"I guess feeling comfortable is helpful for opening up, so it makes sense. Crazy to think, like, most people that know of me are gonna be pretty surprised about all this. I hardly ever talk. It's mostly just making moves for the future—there's always so much going on outside, too. Time for me to actually compose something. Even if I come across like a somewhat dramatic, self-loathing nut at times."

"You do not need to be concerned if people perceive it as dramatic. The only person that fully understands your situation is yourself and you have an interesting story. I think it's great that you're sharing it."

"Yeah, you're right. Foolish of me to believe I could convey it to everybody, though, you know? I know that people generally won't care much, but I still feel the need to do this, regardless."

"I think that those exposed to it will grasp it, as I have."

"Thank you. Let's hope so."

Clears throat

Sips water

"Ready whenever you are."

"All right, so I was …

PHASE I

INGRAINED DAMAGE

Blue Nostalgia

Battling amnesia.
Looking up. Neck bent outta shape. Cerulean
sky showcasing clouds visible.
The wispy sort.
Caught stooped around sundown listening to graceful
church bells, songbird chirps, and wind chime melodies.
The sweet kind.
I'm told it's one day at a time, but already
envision myself as a different entity.
Of the fruitful class.
Until then, just a kid in the basement.
Of the lost nature.

It was just us, a whole family strolling home from Sunday mass in a relatively calm village. The gang consisted of myself, four of my six older siblings, and my parents, Theresa and Neil. Following church services, we traditionally enjoyed endless stacks of mom's delicious pancakes, shot hoops in the driveway, and played PlayStation 2 games in the basement, in that exact order. We were a usual, diverse, and lively family. During those free days, we were blessed with the gift of complete togetherness. It was genuine peace and genuine tranquility that fully enveloped my innocent mind. As far as I was concerned, I had everything a kid could have wanted from life.

A blissful childhood continued just like the story modes in our favorite video games as I began making friends at school and establishing myself well by playing T-ball across town. The most interesting facet of my life was being able to witness my older siblings develop and essentially make a name for themselves in the community. I emulated each of them closely, like any young kid, because to me, they were the most captivating people around. Due to the twelve-year age difference between me and my second-eldest brother, Jason, I had to come to grips with the fact that they were all so much further ahead in their positions with school and social lives. This was oddly difficult for me to process, as I did not want them to leave the house we'd made so many unforgettable memories in and around.

My father is an avid golfer, a former professional. There were plenty of astounding qualities about our family years ago, aside from the absurd amount of groceries we plowed through, but perhaps the most astounding event of the late 2000s was when my father won one of our state's open golf championships. He arrived home with a trophy, and I did not think much of it because of how uneducated and carefree I was. His candid photograph and victory article were in the local newspaper, and although very impressive, all I recognized was the man who made me take naps during peak baseball time outside. Moreover, in first grade, I recall being introduced to two more older siblings, his children from his previous marriage. Their names are Stacy and Scottie, and they're both British, as my father had traveled to Europe to pursue a professional sports career after college graduation and eventually fell in love "across the pond." I stretched the truth a bit earlier. In reality, the most astounding event of the late 2000s was learning that I had family members no one else I knew had: siblings with a

British accent. To this day, it's probably the most interesting thing about me.

The true beauty of my childhood years lay in the social situations of early grade school. It was at this time that I did not mind going to school. Typically, class sizes consisted of no more than fifteen kids, so you knew everybody, and everybody knew you. Reflecting on the memorable moments in class, but more importantly recess, it was found that I was my pure, defenseless self, never having a guard up because I simply had nothing to guard against. Through fickle reminiscing, suddenly mediocre memories morph into magnificent ones. We all wish we could relive them, don't we? Even in a chapter or two.

My submissive, but comically smooth charisma shone through to classmates, and vivid communal memories are held in high regard because I know the other individuals in my grade feel the same way. The eventful scenes we all took so seriously then exist only in our memories now. Intense, grin-filled playground kickball tournaments are the type of minute memory you recollect from such a long time ago, but without ceasing to wonder if the people you shared them with think about them, too. Bittersweet nostalgia. Just grateful the past has color.

This study cannot progress further without appropriately acknowledging the unfathomably wild summer our family enjoyed in 2008. My father was fresh off his tournament victory, we had a special road trip across the country planned to visit my aunt and uncle, and Jason had just graduated from high school. All was well with the world through my lens. The distant adventure was beyond amusing and gave our family plenty of time to bond with Jason's girlfriend, Emma. Since Jason represented us so profoundly, everybody loved him growing up. I remember the crowded pool parties we hosted in our backyard that seemed to last forever. There were so many of his high school friends at our compact A-frame house, and all I knew how to do was throw accurately, so I pitched to them for hours and was mesmerized by how far they could launch tennis balls beyond our property line's fence. To be completely honest, everything mesmerized me that summer. The world around seemed to unlock its portals, and I'd be hard-pressed to find that sense of camaraderie our town had that summer elsewhere.

The extraordinary season was drawing to an abrupt close, unfortunately, and I'd reluctantly begun stuffing deluxe bags of Cap'n Crunch and Lucky Charms cereal into Jason's duffels before he went to an out-of-state university to study engineering. The abundance of graduation parties I attended during those few months provided me with motivation for the upcoming school year, but the realization of my older brother leaving the house unsettled me in deeper ways than I thought possible. It was bound to happen, but my entire childhood up to that point had a distinct glowing blue hue, and it would surely become a bleaker shade of gray, even though I felt content with where things were at my young age. Little did I know that my pure, defenseless self who loved to showcase personable traits and field baseballs at recess as if it were my last day on earth would not soon reemerge after familial events that took place following the dreamlike summer defining my youth.

Tension

With Jason attending school away, dealings around the house shifted, but I went about my usual business at school, as Millie had. She and I were the only kids still attending private grade school at the time. When 2009 rolled around, it suddenly became clear that my father and brother Eli were engaged in heated arguments in and around the house that always escalated quickly. The arguments began fiery and ended fiery. The arguments began thunderously and ended thunderously. The arguments began to polarize our household and ended up polarizing our household. It was not the slightest bit unusual to return home from an arduous school day at three o'clock and take refuge in fear behind our couch because of the electric shouting matches and door-slamming episodes by five o'clock. Millie and I witnessed the brunt of the fighting. Sympathizing with her came naturally in the jungle-like situation because she was mature enough to understand more of what was transpiring before us. As a result of the turmoil, the police were contacted on numerous occasions. My mother was under duress, and increased flanking pressure from my brother Jordan came into play. The house-wide conflict did not include two parties, but four. My parents never seemed to see eye to eye on pivotal topics, and neither did Jordan and Eli. Jordan's growing frustration with Eli contributed to his basement migration from their shared upstairs loft and ultimately his exit from our home altogether.

Tension. All the pressure. It's what Millie and I grew accustomed to existing within as familial matters progressed and worsened. Naively, I recall thinking that the absence of Jason in our home may have triggered the downfall of my parents' relationship. Not sure what else I was to think as a seven-year-old lad. My father worked the third shift, so sleep and argument schedules were atypical yet ruthlessly consistent. With Eli out of our abode, the troublesome area of the marriage was now cemented in the interrelationship of my parents and Jordan. The disagreement consolidation, living in the basement at the time, further amplified the emotional forces in our living space. It was almost as if I could cut the tension in the kitchen with the butter knife I used on my toast while preparing for school and take cover from the sharp utterances being exclaimed with my blanket while preparing for any night's sleep, as well. You see, the dial controlling the status of relentless fighting seemed to have been adjusted beyond its capability within the four walls—to eleven, if you will. All hours of the day presented a possibility of aggressive behavior, and even physical threats were not off the table. Completely immersed in a broken living environment, I humbly wondered if matters could steep lower. Turned out, they could.

What's that cliché saying? "When one door closes, another one opens." Ironically, in this scenario, the close of the first decade of the twenty-first century and the opening of the 2010s reflected the timeline of the relationship. The year 2010 represents the beginning of the severance of the cordial relationship, with the marriage having begun in the year 2000. Somewhere amid the emotional warfare, I had officially heard the last door slam as my mother officially filed for divorce and demanded that my father find a place to live elsewhere.

Upon my return home from one of the final school days of the second grade, I decided to test my luck by entering my parent's room despite the fleeting potential to witness more live and in-person unpleasant discourse. Opening the creaky, ungreased door, I noticed my mother getting ready to leave the house alone. I scurried to take a load off on the bed, but my attempt proved feeble as more emotional information was loaded on. She said calmly, "He's moved into an apartment across town, and you have to pack some things up so you can head to school from his place in the morning." Although this specific scene is ingrained in my mind, I do not recall what I stated next in its entirety.

shakes head

Amnesia.

Anyway, the conversation confused me plenty. So much so that it caused me to fall into a worrisome mental state that I had never experienced before. My mother's comforts were to little avail, because I was still stressing as my father picked me up that evening. The thoughts commanding my mind were more attached to the logistics of the night's stay and early morning school preparation than the status of our family's fundamental flaws and transgressions. Having rarely spent a night under any other roof, it was an abrupt adaptation to make. Unbeknownst to me before uncovering the obscurities of my past, I'd never attributed the ominous bedroom conversation to initiating the worrisome thought episodes to be dispersed between the lines of my existence afterward.

"Two minutes left to finish your quizzes!" announced our teacher as the school year lingered on. Glancing up from my paper, I quickly realized that I had not gotten anywhere near completing the quiz. I zoned out. Even knowing that I had to hurry did not eliminate any of the highly unfamiliar worrisome thoughts infiltrating my mind. An abnormal gut-dropping sensation inhibited me from processing the grammar quiz in front of me. It may seem like a minor occurrence, but the sudden change in familial matters affected more than my ability to perform in school with mental fogginess and uneasiness. The worrying did not cease as the summer of 2010 progressed. If we had a rubber ball game at 6:00 p.m., you best believe I was fully dressed with cleats on by 9:00 a.m. It was not because I loved baseball that much, but because the constant flow of unsureness washed over me at an overwhelming rate. Teammates would question why I had all my gear at the ready thirty minutes before the first pitch, having no idea that I'd been watching television on the couch all day wearing my town-representative gold uniform. Absolutely bizarre and utterly ridiculous. I know.

Returning to my father's old yellow muscle car after practice one overcast fall afternoon, I sensed something odd about his aura. Not knowing the reason for the difference in the slightest, he gently pulled out a white plastic container from a Walmart bag on his side of the car. I asked, "You get a new phone? What happened to the LG?" Because he was concerned about my mother's future custody tactics, he answered, "I got this for you so we can stay in contact. I want you to keep this away from your mother." Without asking many more questions, I snatched the device and decided to obey the order while being dropped off at the house. Having ascended to the loft after sharing a room with Millie all my life, I contemplated the ideal position to store the Tracfone while I was home and at school as if it was all some form of espionage. The contemplation resulted in me placing it inside my backpack's inner compartment during the day and pillowcase at night. For an adequate amount of time, my mother was oblivious to the phone's existence. Possession of the minute-regulated device was the first of many concealment orders I was given at a young age. I began to become slyly quick-witted, not only at home, but in school, too. Although I was the quieter type of boy in class, I continued to expand my social circle and laugh endlessly with my two closest friends. Our humor blending was enough to preserve my happiness most days. On the flip side, pretending everything was just fine to seem normal among classmates gripped me tightly by 2011.

Radioactive Fallout

Thankfully, the town I first grew up in offered me more distractions than I knew what to do with. I eagerly took advantage of the many baseball diamonds, popular skateboarding spots, and most notably, the elementary school playground about a hundred yards north of our house. The open recreational area next to the playground is often the place my mind wanders to whenever I dream of my original hometown. To escape from matters out of control, and certainly, out of my control, I'd spend entire afternoons alone in that courtyard with a baseball bat, tossing tennis balls to myself and hitting them at the school's wall in anticipation of them bouncing back to me, just to do it all over again ten seconds later. Losing practically every usable tennis ball I could get my hands on to the vast roof, I consistently had no choice but to return home. By the third and fourth grades, my parents trusted me enough to leave me to my ventures alone in the neighborhood. Thank goodness, because even though I was becoming more well-received by my classmates, I much preferred to fly solo.

Not a complete outcast, I cherished the opportunity to stay at friends' houses and travel on minitrips with them, like a usual kid. After leaving these homes, a single emotion surfaced without fail: the shock. The shock that I seemed to trail my friends socially by about five years. The shock that their parents' in-laws could show up in their kitchen unannounced and not have a fresh police report filed by the end of the evening. The shock that all the guys and gals I grew up alongside had families that coexisted enough to help them with math homework following a scrumptious home-cooked meal any given night. I grew envious of their situations, and that creeping envy morphed into a formidable desire to isolate myself along with my developing pain. *Why pay visits to smoothly operating households in the community knowing the only thing you have to look forward to is returning home to a quarter of the family you formerly resided with?* I was fed up with the awkward, nearly unbearable law enforcement welfare visits, as well. On too many occasions, I'd be midway through a

Gran Turismo 5 race on the PlayStation 3 and hear knocks at the front door by the local policeman, who I'm sure was agitated by the weekly calls to check on a relatively self-sufficient boy home alone doing no more harm to himself than burning ramen noodles in the microwave. I acknowledged the checks were organized for good reasons, but that did not ease any troubles. Trapped in the middle of a much more complicated war, I was not the only one over all of it emotionally, but the ripple effects were not finished in their displacement.

While the sun began to set on a humid and hazy summer night, my father and I were wrapping up one of our hour-long discussions over the Tracfone I continued to keep secret. Well, it wasn't a discussion. It was a speech he gave regularly on the unfortunate details regarding his marriage conspiracy theories and reconciliation attempts with my mother. I said, "Goodnight, Dad," and lay in bed counting how many words I managed to get in the entire call. Narrowing it down to about eight or nine, I understood that the strain of the divorce process weighed heavy on him, and he was venting to me and the next-door neighbors to cope with the hurt. My heart broke for him with each newsbreak, but everybody else in my immediate family sided with my mother strongly. Furthermore, while other kids my age chilled at home, I occasionally chilled at the marriage counselor's office while my parents hashed it out in the adjacent room. Smacking on the Jujubes I grubbed together from their counselor's desk, I thought to myself, *Man, this has just got to end*. Events of this nature did not exclusively occur in a professionally tended setting, though. I remember nights at my father's apartment with my mother present that included aimless small talk and a consuming a bounty of party-size chip bags. Even at age nine, I recognized the irreconcilable relationship further unraveling before my eyes.

I caught wind of the divorce finalization notice and took a defeated stroll a block west of our house, where my father typically picked me up discreetly. Adjusting my head from being fixed on the cracked sidewalk, I saw him leaning outside of his coupe dressed in a suit. We shared an intimate moment, certainly one that I'll never forget. Man, the looks we gave each other. Embracing him, I heard sobs for the first time. The marriage was officially dissolved, but the fallout of the legal and spiritual decisions made that sweltering afternoon remains radioactive.

The severance of my parents' cordial dealings had taken place, but I felt the need to persevere through every uncomfortable situation I was confronted with. Obviously, there were some considerable shortcomings within the communication department of the divorce finalization. Without applying, I had assumed the role of a third-party messenger who was responsible for relaying all messages to my parents, who practically despised each other, no matter the level of importance. Situationally, things were tender, and weighty baggage was placed on my shoulders. I had the feeling that indefinitely was the placement, too.

"Just pull in on the right side of the street and we'll unload the truck from there!" bellowed my uncle as we were unloading my father's belongings into his newly rented basement further south, a ten-minute drive from our hometown. His apartment lease had ended, and he needed to rent a cheaper place. Also, it was closer to his work, so he jumped at the opportunity to move in. At this point, I was used to rapid changes, and the new scenery did not fluster me as I was already fond of the more densely populated city to which he had moved because I'd played a couple of baseball seasons there.

The warm months of 2013 brought warm memories. Swim sessions, friends' birthday parties, and increased freedom in town thawed my partially frozen mind swiftly. In addition to that fun, my father advised me of the week-long trip we'd soon take to touch base with Stacy and Scottie across the Atlantic. I anticipated that adventure patiently through the excitement of what would be my first overseas plane ride. Before we left the States, I had swimming to do. You could not have kept me out of our backyard pool that summer if you tried. As I practiced my inefficient doggy paddle, my mother swam over to me, and we began conversing in a laid-back manner. Without warning, she informed me that she was pregnant. "Wai ...What?" I responded in a bewildered trance. I simply did not know what to think or say. Essentially what I took from our aquatic dialogue was that I would no longer be the youngest sibling and that Millie, my mother, the baby, and I were moving to a different house, about ten miles northwest of our hometown, at the end of August.

The massive bombshell unnerved me while living my final weeks at home, not only because I was unsure where "home" was going to be anymore, but because the sympathy I felt for my father became more potent with each passing day. My worry skyrocketed as the trip approached, mostly due to the task I had to educate him about the relocation almost immediately. Communication and emotional stability were so mediocre that while we were in the United Kingdom, the main thought wreaking havoc in me was the knowledge of the increased distance my father would need to travel once I was living in the different county. The toll it took on me was monumental, and I could only imagine the feelings my two siblings had to cope with during the trip, too. Considering the circumstances, the general vibe of our father was cold and disturbed. It was difficult to enjoy our fellowship. My father seemed confused and fatigued from jet lag and working overtime incessantly. We three children distracted ourselves with recreational activities like basketball, table tennis, and searching for street food. Alas, we were all tapped out emotionally, and my blues increased tenfold as I witnessed my father seem to hit rock bottom. But at least we were together.

The 737 touched down back home in early August and having delayed unleashing the intelligence bombshell to my father as long as I could, I told him sternly as if I were ripping off a bandage. He was just as shocked as I was when I found out about the move. Our minds were on the same wavelength through the situation, but he believed resisting the plan was crucial to my life's success. I was not exactly sure of that, because I was not done processing the idea of being an older brother, leaving the only town I knew for a nearby opposing school, abandoning my friends when things looked optimistic, and residing in the country when I was more of a city kid. My mind activity was chaotic and perplexing, but there was no time for feelings because we needed to pack and repair some imperfections in our house before moving. Fully expecting the worst from my transfer into fifth grade as my self-esteem plummeted, I also suspected continued fallout from the nuclear war of a divorce would be present while I adjusted to school nearby, tiptoeing around it temporarily or not. My mental health took a back seat on the drive, and although it was in critical condition, I kept it secret. Only time would tell if I could navigate through radiation from the relationship's bitter end, and if prospering was possible despite the dark clouds looming overhead.

To you, Son,
I'm with you today.
I'll be with you tomorrow.
The downpours, along with the strife.
—*God*

Mind Relics: Series I

1. "A word fitly spoken is like apples of gold in pictures of silver" (Proverbs 25:11).
2. "Look into their minds, at what the wise do and what they don't" (Book 4, #38, *Meditations*).
3. Associating nostalgia with melancholy is fair and logical. The way a melody can transport the mind to a specific moment in time without fail, perhaps a moment considered to be our "glory days," is extraordinary.

   Alas, we cannot go back. They exist now only in our memories.
4. A fruitful work, a structurally sound house to reside in, and a heated rig to haul loved ones. What more could one possibly need out of life, materialistically?
5. If your values and beliefs suggest that what you're witnessing is utter foolishness, there's no sense in partaking in that act. Run from it, even if it costs you the fool's worldly indulgences.
6. You should not become angry at a fool for doing something foolish. That would prove you both fools.
7. Most things in life can be understood through openness and perspective. The behavior of another you've been perplexed with your entire existence could suddenly make perfect sense given the right opportunity and circumstance. It's nearly impossible to grasp a foreigner's way of life when leading a closed, rather isolated life with familiar acquaintances exclusively.
8. With societal normalization attempts increasing exponentially, let's also normalize taking time to think

inwardly and heal through reflection and perspective in various ways without being perceived as doing too much.

9. Not to worry. Only God can judge righteously, being the real "Him."
10. Vain gossip and devised narratives from the outside leave abysmal room for honest work. No need to be a part of those empty agendas.
11. It's one day at a time. We cannot possibly take life any other way. Stringing together successful weeks through hard work leads to successful years, then successful decades, and before we know it, we've lived successful lives.
12. Life's balanced rhythm and tempo are meaningful and different for every person. Find yours and flow on your journey steadfastly.
13. "Your ability to control your thoughts—treat it with respect. It's all that protects your mind from false perceptions—false to your nature, and that of all rational beings. It's what makes thoughtfulness possible, and affection for other people, and submission to the divine" (Book 3: In Carnuntum, #9, *Meditations*).
14. If it's worth doing, it's worth doing right. It's worth doubling down for and worth surpassing surface-level visions for.
15. You are special and a glow to this world, so allow yourself to shine. God has a purpose for everybody and has provided us with unique charms to be used for good. You never have to ask for the courage to use them

because you already possess the courage. You carry much more power than you may realize.

16. What's worse? Spending your fleeting time on this planet alone, or spending it with those who make you feel alone?
17. For yourself, fight fire with fire and you'll only further agitate the deep wound. Fight fire with pure water and it may never develop into a scar.
18. It's commonly expressed that comparison is the thief of joy. Correct. Prevailing in a meaningless comparison test with a neighbor will result in temporary happiness, but remember, what we're seeking is long-term, freeing joyfulness.
19. Believe in young aspiring prospects. The willingness to surrender one's own pride and instill knowledge in the minds of the next generation is conducive to great growth in the future.
20. Having trouble distinguishing dreams and nightmares from reality. Today's world is susceptible to circumstances more bizarre and outlandish than the wildest of unconscious brainwaves. With sane feeling crazy and crazy feeling sane, trust and attention must be placed in faith and not of the flesh.
21. You spend your entire conscious existence in your head, so work to make it a place you do not mind inhabiting. That's sense, sure, but is it common?
22. When it's ringing, answer the call of your mental health at once before any other senseless outside expectations flood your mind corruptly. Know the difference between what's real and what thoughts are unsolicited.

23. Pray for your family. Pray for your friends. Pray for the people you thought were your friends. We're all just trying to make it in this life. It's best not to tread troubled waters, though.
24. Difficult to imagine the rich thinking about money on their deathbeds. Money may buy you sorts of happiness, but void-filling everlasting peace of mind is too precious for a price.
25. Everything manifesting in your life will naturally occur in good health and in due time. Be patient and ensure you're ready for the blessings to be bestowed upon you.
26. Nothing is ever random. Strange happenings occur all the time, but only one authority knows precisely what's what. Fear Him.
27. "Whereas ye know not what shall be on the morrow. For what is your life? It is even a vapour, that appeareth for a little time, and then vanisheth away" (James 4:14).
28. Keep watch for snakes in your garden. Trouble is, they're so maniacal the likelihood of spotting one before it bites is slim to none. Nevertheless, we push forward.
29. Success in life is near, not far. You must strike a robust balance of opposites in as many areas as possible to achieve it, however.
30. Let doubters and discouragers doubt and discourage. Relinquish the desire to clear up futile, untrue rumors about yourself if you notice any. Calmness is worth far more to you than stressing about the abysmal chance that you get through to those who do not even value their own words.

31. Wake up from any trances and assume full control of the life you promised yourself. Our ability is ever diminishing, and time is ticking, so we cannot afford to waste more years hibernating. We were not created for that, yet many individuals choose to do nothing at the inflated cost of their most capable decades on earth.
32. Release deep-rooted sewage you hold captive in your mind, for it is merely hazardous waste weighing you down and preventing your takeoff.
33. If it's clarity you seek to find, distance yourself from the world's folly and accept the answers in the silence—the loudest silence you may ever hear.
34. The final exhale you sigh before sleep provides more than enough information. Interpret and compartmentalize it accordingly.
35. Unlock your past to lock up your future.

[Therapy—11:47 a.m.]

"The best part hands-down has to be the conversations I have with others nowadays. Just relating on a similar wave and laughing with people I otherwise would've never spoken to. And you could work next to someone your entire career and not know who they really are. Concealment is sketchy."

"More often than not, individuals with cases like yours feel ashamed of how they'd be perceived if anyone caught wind of their struggles."

"Exactly. You know what, though, I wouldn't have wanted it to be all that different. Every problem, every pain got me to this point, and it's beautiful."

"I see. You really wouldn't change much of anything about your endeavors?"

"Uh, I mean, if I could go back and do it differently, I would've slid into home. I would've held on to my dawgs longer, too. Egotistical. So disconnected constantly … like a robot or something."

shakes head

exhales deeply

"OK. That's an interesting way of putting it. Was there a particular moment when you realized you were not being your best or who your younger self would be proud of?"

"Yeah. Being alone speeds up that realization process. Regret and rage sink in involuntarily, but positioning yourself better emotionally is never involuntary—it's so difficult, you know. Feeling like I'm gonna need back pay for the few years I missed …

smirks

because I'm back."

"Your energy with this is compelling. Let's keep going."

"Yeah, for sure. Are you hungry? I'm ordering some Thai food and a few Persian donuts."

"No thanks, I'm fasting 'til dinner tonight."

"Ahh, well, I'll get more. You'll change your mind when you see these donuts."

PHASE II

INKLINGS OF NEUROSIS

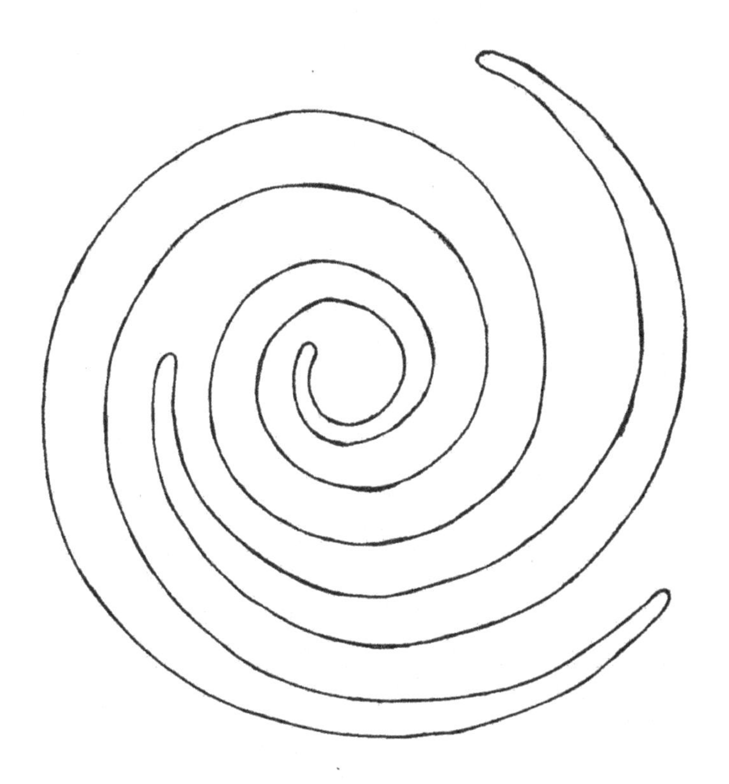

Fugazi

Trying not to drop my refreshing mint Oreo ice cream dessert and contribute to the collection of carpet stains, I pressed snugly against a bulky bunk bed ladder in the third row of our trooper of a Dodge Caravan, the same van our family drove cross-country and back. With help from Rick, my mother's partner, we sardine-packed most of our essential belongings well. Millie had just obtained her probationary driver's license, so fortunately or unfortunately, she was behind the wheel. Headed west on a narrow back road on a gorgeous afternoon, the four of us spotted a red SUV and a navy-blue sedan parked alongside the ditch. It was late August, so roadside vegetation was overgrown and tick ridden. As I enjoyed the final spoonful of the soft serve, I heard Millie and my mother scream in unison, "What are they doi- Oh my goodness!" Their reactions were warranted, as I rotated and saw two grown people having sexual intercourse about a yard and a half from the tarmac between the two vehicles. I could not believe my eyes. We all chose to laugh it off, but I remember thinking, *Is this type of thing typical here? Just people rendezvousing on roadsides and doing unspeakable things to each other next to farmer's crops? What!?* It's times like these when you wish you'd just taken the main roads. Honestly, finding it fitting for that ingrained scene to be my maiden memory in our new hometown, I attempted to lighten up as Millie and I had orientations for our respective schools approaching quickly.

The brief car ride to the elementary school I'd attend

for the open house registration was nerve-racking. Every considerable component of life had been severely altered. Education was the last thing I wanted to expend energy on because I knew my parents would be in the same room for the first time since the divorce, so on the horizon could be a hostile first impression with my new teachers and classmates. Settling into our corner classroom, I casually used the word "belligerent," an adjective I'd heard from Eli and did not understand, in a sentence to sound smart. My teacher looked at me like, "Yep, all right. This kid is going to be the weird one." As I placed my pencil case and spiral notebooks in my assigned desk neatly, I could not help but note that the rift between my parents could not have been further apart. Just as they ended, I was to begin my journey in a new environment. They went their separate ways that afternoon, but I reservedly suspected a legal saga would sprout.

I weighed 74.6 pounds in early fifth grade. The emotional load I lugged around reluctantly was far heavier. My appetite suffered a dip as winter slashed through. The mere thought of eating lunch at school made me nauseous most days, so I stuck to a hearty lunch of oyster crackers and chocolate pudding. Contributing almost nothing to daily classroom and cafeteria conversations, I felt very distant from my classmates maturity-wise. Not dealing with a split home and having a child support dollar worth on their heads, let alone knowing what it was specifically, set them apart from me. Upon completion of my one gram of protein, 250-calorie lunch, like clockwork, I'd look down at my hands to see purple abrasions on the upper sides of my ring fingers from subconsciously rubbing my pinkies over them for weeks. Friends often looked at them and asked why they had a frostbitten appearance. In addition to the abrasions, I bit my nails and skin, stuttered, and developed uncontrollable eyelid and eccentric shoulder shrug twitches. Shamefulness entered my mind then and there. I was ashamed of the circumstances regarding our move to a different school district already but coupled with the sprouting mental and physical effects, the variables could have only produced a socially awkward, timid, and chronically depressed boy at school with diminishing self-esteem.

After I finished the booklet containing material I'd already learned and applied at private grade school, my teacher tapped me on the shoulder and discreetly sent me to the school's counseling office. The walk to the office was strikingly similar to the defeated stroll I took to meet my father once the divorce was finalized. With my hand over my face, I thought, *Fantastic, here we go again*, and once I sat down in the counselor's office, we engaged in small talk that made me feel like I was in the second grade again. "What's your favorite candy bar?" she asked. "Twix or Snickers?" I said, "Probably Snickers," but I understood that even one of those delicious candy bars could not satisfy me. You see, I was a compliant child up to this point, but I was not having this counseling stuff at all. I had no malice toward the counselor, as she was simply doing her job, but I later discovered that she'd been tasked with keeping tabs on me upon my father's request. My frustrations with aimless welfare interruptions had officially reached their limit. I was done talking to policemen and counselors, so I advised my father to cease his checking efforts for good. The charade to blend in with my "normal" classmates and maintain a low profile was nearly impossible to pull off when drawn out of the conformed crowd, or shadow, intermittently.

"You OK, man? You look like you could cry," my friend asked. I replied swiftly, as if I was surprised to get that question. "Yeah, uh—yeah, I'm fine," I said, with a slight twitchy shoulder shrug to follow. The ability to fully conceal my emotions was not developed, so I fielded those caring questions fraudulently. Every day became an acting performance for which I was not compensated because the disposition of my eleven-year-old self was too unfiltered to land the part. Knowing this, I figured it was more beneficial to isolate myself and drastically reduce the odds of me being caught vulnerable and sullen. Failing to learn how to play guitar and enjoying video games became my primary activities outside of school, as well as the rare occurrence of hanging out with my few closest friends. Influenza kicked me for a week as winter came, adding to my struggle with controlling worrisome thoughts and stress regarding missed schoolwork. The way my mind raced over every little detail, you would have thought the world was ending. I knew there were people around who could offer varying levels of support, but I desired nothing more than to be alone. Alone to wonder where the silver lining to all of this was, alone to discover new ways to cope with the worrisome and depressive impairments that were causing the fugazi I'd been displaying, and alone to not feel the need to display a front in the first place.

War Torn

On an absurdly frigid December morning later that year, Jordan drove Millie and me to a distant hospital in his ancient extended cab truck to see our mother and our newborn sister, Rose. After riding a lavish elevator to the fourth floor, I laid eyes upon Jason, Emma, and Eli, whom I had not seen for ages. We all took memorable pictures together with Rose and enjoyed each other's company, because every one of us led a vastly different life than two years prior. Jason and Emma wanted to snag some grub, so I tagged along to a fast-food restaurant across the bustling expressway. While chatting with them, I received a phone call from my father. "I'll pick you up at the hospital tonight. The Globetrotters are playing in town. OK, son?" I then responded in a confused way because I had no idea that we made those plans, and my mother was not exactly in a capacity to argue through the tender situation as she'd given birth less than twelve hours earlier. Without the strength or wherewithal to decline, I simply ended the call, fearing the tension and drama was sure to rise as the discontent messenger in a precarious situation. When asked about things by my siblings, seldom did I tell them the truth in full. Social distance was the name of the game for me. So, I sat slouched on the rock-hard bedside couch in room 412 all night avoiding the pending issue and supporting my mother, which was a dynamic route, because I could not hang around her side of the family without being subjected to the bashing of my father's name. A heightened sense of shame clouded my mind to the most positive thoughts about myself, and stings caused me to have a much stronger sense of empathy for loved ones like my parents.

The gut feeling: a natural human instinct. Do you obey yours? I did in early 2014 as I felt the magma simmer beneath the slowly hardening crust of the divorce. To illuminate, the relationship I had with my father was intact. The only formidable threat posed to us occurred when any member of my mother's side mixed into our dealings. Additionally, Neil had been searching for a new church to attend consistently since 2011. Following a spring worship service, he began sharing his plotted legal arrangements with me. "I want what's in your best interest. You'll be appointed a guardian *ad litem* to represent you, because I think you're better off living with me," Neil stated passionately on our drive to his place. I never knew what to say besides "OK, yeah." I was never opposed to living with Neil, but I also did not want to hurt my mother or my siblings in any way, either. Before preparing for his night shifts, Neil and I often discussed intimate details of his financial outlook and feelings in his basement, which further contributed to my rising stress levels as I was exposed to the inner workings of both the frightening legal and emotional aspects of the custody battle from a father's perspective. I knew precisely what would be on the line come court time.

Discussing upcoming courtroom moves was not the only extracurricular activity I participated in, however. To assist in distracting my mind, I continued to play Little League baseball for a nearby organization. Returning to play with a select few old friends was beyond awkward to me. We'd play long toss in the outfield, then field groundballs in orderly lines that brought about difficult conversations. "Why did you leave us?" a former classmate asked. I answered him reluctantly, "I—I just had to go." It shattered me to see the confusion in my dawgs' eyes. From that point on, I wondered if my life could ever be relatable or understood by my peers. Having one foot in the door in our new town while the other was still in the original town was only making matters more complicated, and I now had this parent-picking dilemma looming in front of me.

Just as I dreaded telling my father about us moving, I dreaded "spilling the beans" to my mother about his custody tactics. Tell me, how is a kid supposed to take vital placement exams seriously with ultrapressurized thoughts inhabiting their conscience without any warning? Eventually, my mother caught wind of the custody suit from her attorney and countered with an effort to withhold any joint custody of me. So, there I was, engrossed by the blunt knowledge that my young fate rested in the fact that I could either live fully with my father or only see him on rare, agreed-upon occasions, or maybe never. With everything that transpired since 2009, if there was one thing I knew, it was that anything could happen at any given moment. A missile was my part in the war, evidently, so I began warning fellow classmates that I may not return for the succeeding school year as we signed each other's yearbooks, similarly to what I'd proclaimed in the fifth-grade orientation just a year earlier at the previous school. I grew especially fond of the boys and girls I met that year, and it hurt me and others to say, but I needed to be disconnected enough to not be emotional if my father was granted full custody. There was not a second to spare for vulnerability.

Precisely as my father prophesied, the time had risen to provide a statement to my guardian *ad litem*. While I conversed in the drab conference room with him, my brain seemed to freeze, and I answered the surface-level questions with unrealistic positivity as if I could outsmart a psychiatric professional with ease. I thought, *This is so pointless*, while continuing to ingest questions that I did not know the answers to because I was submerged in a place in which I had to choose which caring parent I'd rather live with. The love I have for them would and could never cease, regardless of how daunting and hideous the postmarital affairs proved to be.

Results from the heated battle had surfaced. Both my parents had been denied their respective requests, which essentially meant a whole lot of nothing. Nothing. Nothing changed after all that expensive confusion. Thankfully, I was granted freedom to see Neil whenever I pleased. After all that time, the figurative bleeding had stopped. I now had the opportunity to develop with my newly made friends, which forced me to sever past connections, for the time being. Through the madness, a colder, more disconnected kid appeared with fresh-featured psychological capabilities: adaptability and skilled suppression of deeply rooted feelings. A new legal revelation, a new town, and new powers arose from the darkness just before the infamous years of junior high school. Perfect timing.

Try Harder

Spiritual nourishment: the gift that my father had been hoping and praying for since the collapse of the slippery court ordeals. He and I grasped it the moment we sat in the pews at a neighborhood Bible church. Every member of the congregation welcomed us with open arms as we were, producing a comforting feeling that had been awfully dormant in our lives for years. Suddenly, he began to delve into the Bible and studied the Book of Proverbs most dominantly. I often noticed him fast asleep with it on his chest when I woke him for overtime night shifts. I felt too young to extract the scriptures' wisdom, but I went along to church most Sundays to help heal not only his wounds, but mine, too. It was evident that we'd found our home there. Anyway, overtime was my father's middle name in 2015 and 2016, as he had piled up a scary amount of credit card debt and needed to claw his way back into the black, if you will. Although my frontal cortex was already beginning to overcompensate, his presence calmed me when it was simply him and I together without pressing familial lore on our minds.

Taking a seat in science class after a record-breaking three-touchdown recess football game, I overheard some friends call me a "try hard." The first time I was criticized for it, I was like, "Huh? I extended effort and success was the result, and you're all ragging on me for it?" There was a fundamental understanding that it was merely an ongoing lighthearted joke between us guys, but for whatever reason, it irked me. Actually, I know the reason precisely: pent-up frustration embedded psychologically bubbling upward because I was being made fun of for finally making an effort to grow relationships with classmates. Following years of familial complications and pity, I did not need to embarrass myself more at school, so I stepped away from initiating meaningful friendships as much as possible. Self-doubt, worry, and introversion steadily inhibited me from allowing my natural spirit to shine through to others. Nonetheless, lagging socially was the least of my concerns. Witnessing the family together healed me temporarily, but the chronic blues I was experiencing demanded my attention far more prevalently.

Although I was a scrawny kid about twenty-five pounds underweight, I was not cowardly enough to permit the "try hard" folly to affect my effort in sporting performances. My mind had been altered, but one thing remained rock solid: my passion for baseball. My friend Johnny asked me if I wanted to play for Rocky Ridge, the Little League organization he was an all-star for. Since my high school destination changed, I agreed to join. As the season flew by, I bonded with my new teammates and played well enough to become one of the best players on the team. Since I dreaded most parts of junior high, having the opportunity to escape busywork and stress was incredible, and the players I shared the field with made me laugh harder than I ever thought possible. My dawgs, for real.

"Milo, why don't you come in the living room and be with us? Turn off the game?" my mother asked loudly as I remained secluded from all other human beings in my bedroom. I hollered back, "I can't pause it, Ma! It's online it—ugh." Beyond the usual early adolescent problems, trying to explain to elders that online games cannot be paused is a whole other issue. Over time, it became less of a strain to small talk with Rick and take care of Rose. It took several years, but going home after school was something I looked forward to again. There was never fighting, only the wineglass-blasting cries from baby Rose and the continued creative bashing of my parents' names at both sides of family events. A Christmas party at my father's brother's home usually consisted of drawn-out rants about my mother, and events at our house consisted of jabs at my father, linked together by at least two of my siblings for my ears to hear. They rarely felt like warm fellowship-filled parties as the people I love most were targets of filthy flame. The hints of rage from these gossips snuck into my mind and converted into one goal: gaining control to a degree so unreasonable that it's unfathomable to many people, understandably so.

Before any of us knew it, our stomping grounds defrosted in 2017, and I'd begun exerting more consideration for my future aspirations amid my private affairs. Since purchasing my first vehicle and earning a college degree were in the cards, saving for them was not going to happen unless I started "going hard in the paint," as Jason's close buddy put it. Taking his advice, I had my mother drive me to apply at a fast-food restaurant in a sleepy adjacent town. I landed the esteemed position of cashier there, even though my self-esteem and conversational skills with customers were pitifully atrophic. But you have to start somewhere, I suppose. The mundane cleaning tasks I was assigned were relatively enjoyable for me, which checked out because my friends noticed my creeping germophobic and somewhat hypochondriacal tendencies and pointed them out whenever I refused to shake their hands. "It's cold season!" I'd always say sarcastically to get chuckles, but that was my measly reasoning behind not wanting to contract others' hand bacteria. Stacking lids, cleaning trays, and stocking sauce packets may seem brainless, but I had it down to a science. No customer or acquaintance left that restaurant lobby without an adequate handful of cinnamon starlight mints. Ever. Nah, not on my watch.

You could chalk it up to me being peculiar, but I deem idiosyncratic to be a more accurate adjective to describe my disposition. My peculiarity took its trip to the most important baseball game of my career in June. With two successful seasons under our belts at Rocky Ridge, I proved to be one of the two foremost leaders on the team. I pitched and played third base exclusively, and it was only on baseball diamonds that I remotely resembled an extroverted person. Arguably, we had the best team since 2015, so confidence and adrenaline were swimming through our veins as we headed into the bottom of the seventh inning.

The night was picture-perfect. There was no wind, no pesky mosquitoes, and no hotdog over two dollars at the concessions. The game was perfect. There was no unfairness, no chirping by either side, and no room for error to land a win. With the boxing match of a championship game tied at 6–6 with two outs and me standing at third following a walk and base advances, I steadied my breathing and focused on the opposition's pitcher, because we took Pony League ball very seriously. Our catcher cracked a sharp ground ball to their pitcher, so I turned on the jets to home plate thinking he would attempt a throw to first base for the force out and end the inning. Shockingly, he decided to relay a dart to their catcher while I pranced toward him. A touch on the plate before his tag meant a walk-off victory for us, but I declined the slide and remained running full-steam into the catcher's mitt at the precise moment I landed on home plate, even though our coach was yelling "Down! Down!" It seemed to be too close to call, but "OUT!" bellied the umpire after the most suspenseful two seconds of our lives. I could not believe it. When I gazed at our bench, I recognized they could not believe it, either. Major doses of inadequacy and shame replaced adrenaline and clouded my pitching performance in extra innings, and I blew the game for us. We lost.

Witnessing the other team pose for photographs with the championship trophies left me falling apart against my father's car in disbelief. I let myself down, I let our fans down, and I let my friends down. There was not another soul on the planet more upset with me than me, though. Only I knew the real reason behind the loss. On top of rarely needing to, I did not want to slide and run the risk of the infield dirt staining my white pants. Yes, you read that correctly. I opted out of sliding into home plate because I did not want to stain my white uniform pants. How absurd is that? One could imagine how much I beat myself up over it as a story more embarrassing would have been difficult for even the most creative writers to devise. About a week removed from my blunder, I texted our team group chat accepting responsibility for the loss while intentionally leaving out the OCD culprit. I learned lessons, but was anything done about my psychological impairments? Negatory. As time progressed, I fell further into the abyss of my pathetic, yet overwhelming issues, and by no means does it take a rocket scientist to understand that a cavernous pit entails a lofty climb out.

Numb

Spending the remaining days of summer 2017 working from one in the afternoon until nine o'clock at night and chilling alone playing video games, I sat back on our couch with NBA 2K17, paused, and thought, *All right, things are looking up. High school starts in a week. I'll play basketball and baseball for school, get my license—things are totally fine.* Both of those wishful thoughts came true as my shell of awkwardness wilted more with each passing month. Obviously, it did not take until freshman year to realize that other students carried themselves differently compared to me, but that concept was solidified every school day while I gently placed my backpack's contents into locker 114 and saw how relatively disorganized and aloof most peers seemed to be.

It's no secret that girls tend to enter young guys' minds more heavily in high school, and I wanted to evolve my appearance to reach a more desirable status. Looking into the mirror one fall evening after a haircut, I slicked my thin, light-brown hair back and to the right in a single swift motion, as opposed to the stale, straight-line combover I'd been rocking with since birth. Even though the styling looked halfway decent, I needed any validation and confidence at all to arrive in algebra sporting it. I deployed mental deliberation, like the meditative process I did while deciding to share these memories, and the result was the 1950s-inspired greaser flow becoming my signature look.

In an afternoon class lecture, I'd been awakened from a deep sleep by my phone's vibration on my thigh. It was a text message from Theresa with a picture of my newborn nephew. Excited to become an uncle, I decided to take notes instead of continuing my slumber. Another reason I was awake and eager was because I had a date with an incredible girl I had just met. Needless to say, the vibes were immaculately euphoric as young love was born. Moving on, my early high school years seemed to progress expeditiously as every part of my life had improved since the custody battle was resolved. A smoother hairstyle, fresh unclehood, and a new girlfriend entered my circle, and they were welcome, especially because my father and I had booked round-trip flights to visit Stacy and Scottie again near summer's end of 2018. The four of us were amped to spend eleven days together because five years earlier, the divorce's embers had yet to cool. For the most part, we were healed thanks to sweet father time.

About a week into the zen, sunlit vacation in the United Kingdom, Stacy, Scottie, and I found ourselves loading stir-fry ingredients and other groceries into Scottie's car before our meal. The absence of our father presented a simpler opportunity to discuss our feelings and reflect on past and current experiences with broken-home living. As we settled for the commute to their aunt's, I opened an enlightening realm conversationally when I questioned, "It could just be me on this, but do you ever notice a stronger sense of empathy for other people? We've been in and around crazy situations and Dad a lot, you know. Just kinda wondering if you both feel that same feeling with awareness around him, I guess." I noticed them process what I asked and simultaneously react energetically to my heartfelt question as if it was an aha moment. "Yes!" they asserted. "It's hard to be with anyone close without being so self-aware and really feeling for people in certain situations, you know?" Scottie added. We continued to reminisce and reflect wondrously until we arrived to prepare sensationally sweet chili-sauced chicken stir-fry, but when we did, our wavelength did not depart from the unbelievable chat we had. Being mature enough to relate with siblings, especially Stacy and Scottie, was freeing, because long-lost pieces were always put in place in their presence. I believe that they are equally as empathetic toward my circumstances as I am to theirs. I cannot help but subconsciously relive my version of their past experiences growing up through their relevant divorce every time I'm with them—neurosis at its most debilitating. All too well did we know the consequences of breaking up. We were exposed early to things we did not want, so you could imagine that we'd have a clear idea of what we do want out of a relationship. It was around the time of this peaceful venture that I realized how toxically warped my view of marriage and having kids became, strictly based on what I'd witnessed and been put through. Surely, the flaws of those marriages would not torment me, of all people, right?

Our return flight was orderly, but it had nothing on the prideful organization of my mind. Brighter days were on the horizon, as I expected to obtain my driver's license in winter, purchase my first vehicle—signaling freedom—and to put the cherry on top, the MLB team we cheer for was headed deep into the playoff series, which had everybody hyped. A corny line would be that "all was right with the world," but it hit the nail on the head, in my case. Since I was in a happy mind state, I joined my friends in whatever they had going on for more fun. Most of them, me included, were at the peak of their desire to be as physically attractive as possible, so weightlifting became the activity we obsessed over. Initially, I deemed it annoying, but grew to thoroughly enjoy getting in shape and occasionally releasing pent-up aggression. Before I knew it, a cheeky license was in my pocket, keys to a trusty (and rusty) five-speed pickup truck were in the ignition, and my girlfriend was riding shotgun. Although my concealment defense mechanisms were operating normally, I permitted most of my true self to glow to her, but not all. I would not dare open up fully so as to seem vulnerable or flawed in any way. I also kept our relationship a secret from my father for about eight months, because I perceived there to be awkwardness and distance between us when girls were the topic of discussion.

My ever-corroding forest green truck needed some rest from time to time, so home life was still at the forefront of my consciousness. Rarely did I complete school assignments at home, but as I did in the spring of 2019, I overheard that Rick was suffering from a severe illness, and it concerned me deeply because this time around, a more unsettling, ominous tone blasted us. Focusing in class, completing regular tasks at work, and maintaining a positive mood proved impossible as his second major battle with cancer went on. Being so hyperaware constantly, I practically lived entire days from Rick's, my mother's, and Rose's perspective while simultaneously attempting to live life on an even keel. I could not help but to psychoanalyze how terrifyingly deep they must have been hurting.

In an absolutely gutting sequence of events, I hopped out of an invigorating shower to a text my mother sent asking me when I'd arrive at the hospital to witness Rick's last breath on the final school day of sophomore year. Shaking my head, gnawing on my fingertips, rubbing my face, and exhaling gravely the entire speedy drive, I tried not to succumb to depression's pull again, but it dripped back into the scene. Sitting at his bedside with Theresa and little Rose beside me, I fell into an emotionless trance until grabbing hold of my mother in support. The moment I embraced her, in tears I began crying out in disbelief for a few moments before wiping my tears on my hoodie, disgusted with myself. Rick passed away that afternoon and Jordan approached me, wondering if I was emotionally stable enough to be dropped off at home alone. I reluctantly answered "Yeah," with the knowledge that the only reason I was emotionally robust enough was after ten years, I'd reached a degree where none of my true feelings were known to anyone externally. I became as cold and as lifeless as the winter we'd recently endured.

Life goes on, but not without every ounce of detriment and pain in your mind and consequently, on your shoulders. Due to my elite emotion-suppression skills, I was not phased noticeably at school or work, although on the inside,

I felt like a neuroticized jumble. There's no conceivable way that any of my teachers, classmates, or teammates had a legitimate concern for me being depressed during those trying times—not a chance. My developed, distant facade prevailed over continuing in my relationship, too. With Rick's sudden passing and the latest baseball season not going well, I hesitantly decided to move on from her before spending a year together. I sensed my mental health plummeting rapidly day by day, and my attitude became indifferent to meaningful relationships I'd been blessed with kindling, including my most promising one. I attempted to explain my situation to her, along with every rigged battle being fought between my ears, but it was to no avail. My extended explanation was an abysmal 10 percent of the grand truth, or, in other words, lies.

The scorching, humid June afternoon of Rick's funeral featured plenty of droplets of perspiration, but not one tear fell from my eyes. It appeared that duct had run dry. Feeling like an automated phony among tearful family members and acquaintances, a serene walk around the river bend accompanied by fresh air sounded wonderful, so I temporarily departed from the celebration of life and stood, slouched, gazing into my somber reflection in the still freshwater. My intrusive thoughts were as follows:

Why am I like this?

What kinds of things will I have to tell Rose when she gets older because of what just happened, and what will she feel when she realizes her older brother has gone crazy?

How much longer can I adequately conceal my feelings and thoughts?

Where do I turn to get the happiness everybody else around me experiences?

When will I stop living the lie that shackles my time on this planet?

I meditated on each of those untamed, but real, questions for a while. As I removed my sunglasses to reveal raw, truthful eyes in the water's reflection, ripples from a kayaker wisped my mirror image into the murky banks.

To you, Son,
I'm with you today.
I'll be with you tomorrow.
The downpours, along with the strife.
This glistening, dichotomous fortune
you are not aware of.
Those people I gave to you … they lost when you lost.
Without feeling and tears, you surely perish and thirst.
—*God*

Mind Relics: Series II

1. "For wisdom is better than rubies; and all the things that may be desired are not to be compared to it" (Proverbs 8:11).
2. "Nowhere you can go is more peaceful—freer of interruptions than your own soul" (Book 4, #3, *Meditations*).
3. A worrisome mind hinders the flawless beauty of exploring your soul and being your true self.
4. Corrupt and unenlightened minds will give in to temptation and worldly pleasures again and again. Not satisfied until obtaining the next best thing per their pride. Consider extending careful teaching to them at the risk of being despised unfairly.
5. Nobody's keeping score except us. The hateful might prey on your downfall, but they do not possess powerful leverage unless you give it to them through weakness.
6. Humble and broken. Questioning memories as if they are merely scars instead—a sound place to heal and grow.
7. Mind only your business and keep the peace. Unless their business becomes yours and threatens your inner peace.
8. This manuscript is in no sense intended to be a victimization campaign, but a celebration of cerebral freeness at the end of a grim tunnel.
9. Seriously ask yourself, *What qualities define my successful future self?* Then take the necessary steps to carry yourself like that revolutionarily powerful

person. You may become that individual sooner than you projected.

10. The needs of the human mind are comparable to the digestive system's needs. It may need to be cleaned, cultured, restrengthened, and evaluated before it's too late.
11. Faith and Love > Greed and Infatuation
12. Although difficult to excavate, tragic memories should be reflected upon and rightly divided to exploit occurrences that interconnect with your current self, tendencies, and mental health status. Do not be afraid or run from imminent pain. Embrace it, along with the story that's been written for you.
13. Simply because you are suffering mentally does not give you the right to use it as justification for continued suffering and means to escape situations prematurely. Know your worth. Do not sell yourself short.
14. The dust settled on our mess. Is it worth ruffling with the pieces strewn about?

    The memories locked away in our mental vaults. Is it worth opening the safes?

    The demons between our ears working tirelessly to keep us up at night. Is it even worth the nightmares? Finally, we might be getting somewhere.
15. Never was able to decide how I felt about the saying, "I liked her so much; I wish I had never met her."
16. Fear blinds us to true perceptions of meaning and purpose in life. Genuine faith will provide a pathway to see yours clear as day.

17. "Keep reminding yourself of the way things are connected, of their relatedness. All things are implicated in one another and in sympathy with each other. This event is the consequence of some other one. Things push and pull on each other, and breathe together, and are one" (Book Six, #38, *Meditations*).
18. Toxic positivity or simply the unfiltered truth?
19. Arrive at conclusions about people based on their character (how they treat people). A far greater observation of worth than their bank account's numerical length.
20. Fortunately, the occurrence of cataclysmic interpersonal events is not required to enable positive change within us. Reflect privately, understand and accept your past, and be the best version of yourself moving into the unknown with humble confidence.
21. Be careful what your mind obsesses and wishes for. You just might receive them.
22. The mind can be a dangerous place. An inside threat. It's able to distort views of what's real and what's not and prevent you from spending any time in your own soul.
23. Melancholy is a variable in this challenging experience, too.

    We must adapt and learn to give thanks for even the worst of days.
24. Better to move out of pure faith than fear. You've lived with your enemy plenty of time, so you of all people possess the willpower to expel it.

25. What good is a hardened heart? A spiteful attitude? A narcissistic complex? What good is any wisdom if concealed for three and a half more scores?
26. Perhaps the toughest battle one fights is with oneself. Strength from confronting and conquering the mind's compromised perceptions develops, and the soul enters the picture for the betterment of those around and the common good.
27. "For to be carnally minded is death; but to be spiritually minded is life and peace" (Romans 8:6).
28. Speak only after thoroughly listening and observing. If you cannot get a word in, you may be surrounded by foolish individuals.
29. Oblivion cannot deliver from problems and difficult truths for long. Haunts and misery will prosper until demons are dealt with courageously.
30. "Not to be driven this way and that, but always to behave with justice and see things as they are" (Book 4, #22, *Meditations*).
31. Cerebral calmness is in many cases low-hanging fruit hidden in plain sight. Cling to the pursuit of it because it is good and by choice confront internal, pending demise to find direction and gain hope for future prosperity.
32. In raw form, social media posts are simply fronts for psychological, physiological, and socioeconomic needs and desires: a cry for help or attention, lust, envy, score-settling, money, greed, relief, vengeance, etc. Safe and appropriate to view them as such.

33. How many more days can any of us afford to loiter in bleak space? Not one. Once out, our cups can and will be filled to overflowing. Debts to society shall be paid back in full, with interest.
34. "Everything's been said before. What could ever be brought to the table?"

    A classic, yet modern-interpretive dish to pass on for the next generation(s) to benefit and glean wise perspectives from.
35. Being lost has a silver lining. It implies that eventually one may be found.

[Therapy—1:54 p.m.]

"I listen to your story and can't help but wonder if you felt as if you were experiencing a life that wasn't yours. Like, were you left shaking your head in the car because of the afflictions or because you believed that you were living someone else's life? Denying the pain as if it was not meant for you?"

"In part, yes. At that time, I just tried to outrun the problems and intrusions in my head as best I could. In um, uh—every public situation, I'd been going through the motions. I'd adapted to viewing my actions and vibe from the point of view of others around me. Kinda appealing to how I expected them to expect me to act and speak—not actually being myself or understanding the reality and truth behind my fronts."

"And those mixed variables produced an element of self-hatred and guilt that kept you from being free or comfortable mentally?"

"Yeah, 100 percent. But you see, it was more complex than that, even. As soon as I thought I solved one problem, another one would arise that was much more powerful. Hardly anything was what it seemed to be for myself and others my age, too, honestly."

"I'll jot that down. We'll definitely touch on that here shortly."

"Yeah, for sure. I'm just hoping we do this thing justice.

slight chuckle

Been playing this scene over and over and over and

know it can be done, even though on paper the balance of what we're trying to convey seems impossible."

"Well, you've managed to keep me guessing so far, so that light hasn't burned out yet."

"Yet… ha ha. Trust me, if someone's gonna mess it up, it's me! We've only covered certain things here—meat 'n potatoes coming up next, though.

glances away

Oh goodness me. I really am seventy-five years old."

shared laughs

PHASE III

NEURO VICES

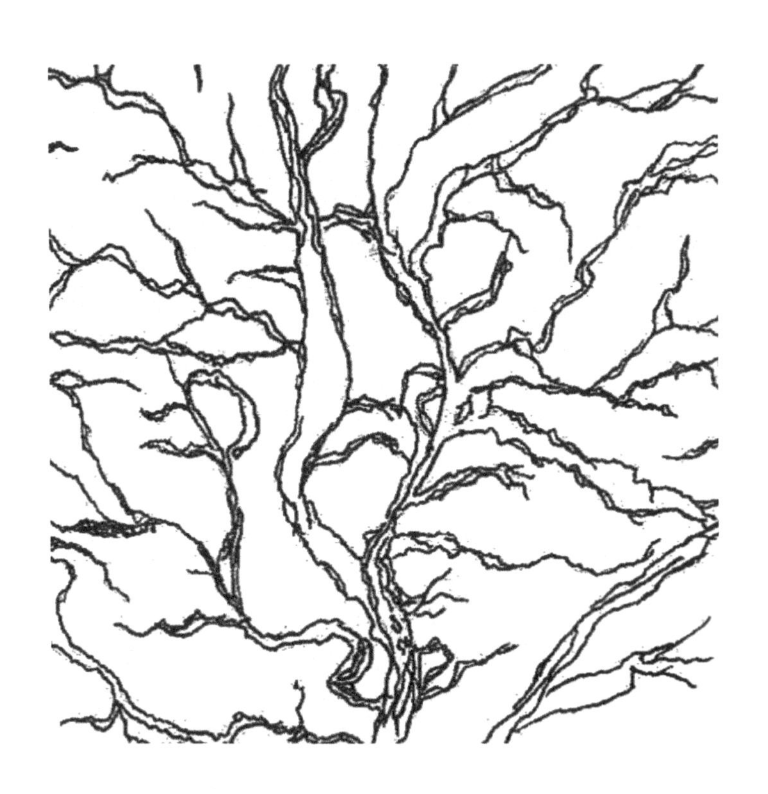

Decoding The Enigma

A vain, eleven-second gaze at himself in the mirror, followed by seven thorough, evenly pressured towel pat-dries. Flowing long hair now, so ten efficient comb strokes toward the north suffice for his liking. Never a hair out of place, never a major external clothing flaw in his eyes. He allows no margin for weakness or meekness, for that matter. There's plenty of margin for reinvention and confidence, though. He strolls down these hallways like he owns the whole district now. You guessed it, only the "cleanest" apparel will do for this one. You will not see him in anything generic, Heaven forbid. Especially following the shopping expeditions he'd gone on after the bitter end of something. This guy has a sour taste in his mouth because of whatever it was. Yes, with the newfound status upgrades he's trying to integrate into his charade, it's evident that a shift has taken place behind the scenes. I try, but I cannot get much out of him. I now know that there's no point in attempting to crack this enigma. Deep down, I know he's got something truthful to profess, something worth more to us than simply being left in that shiny, slicked-back exterior of his. He'll look malnourished one day and the next, his veins will pop like he's in a rage. It's as though he visualizes lanes but does not commit to any of them. What's this guy's game, anyway? Is it to impress the girls in his grade? Is it to be the class clown and entertain now that he has a morsel of fraudulent esteem? Is there a rhyme or reason to why he goes weeks without uttering one word and then preaches monologues religiously to us in the middle of class, for however long he desires? I mean, for goodness' sake, he even steals away a quarter of our teacher's lecture time some days. If only I knew the thoughts running around in his head. Admittedly, if I did know, I'd be able to see if this ordered fool is a straight-up basket case or a calculated artist. See right through him. Either way, something is unraveling in this very classroom. He may just do something he'll regret. I can feel it. No ordinary person obsesses over the things he does to this degree without wild background noise and forces. You tell me, though. Can you catch him?

It's 6:06 a.m. Unilluminated. Six degrees displayed on my nine-inch dashboard infotainment screen. I pull into the vacant parking lot to open the store, per usual for a Saturday. Actually, the lot was not completely vacant. The quiet, oddly convicted team member I manage was already parked and ready for the shift. Even though we both drive similar types of trucks, our mentalities are light-years apart. As I unlock the front door and fire up the grills, he's pestering me about the six minutes' worth of pay he had been deprived of, but I sense a greater rage inside of him. Why does this kid care so much? Every other employee I hire is not like him in any way imaginable. Although he stutters when communicating with customers in my drive-through sometimes, I have no reason to believe he cannot act in an outgoing way. He lets our team delve into his humor and fun-loving nature, but only at his uncommon discretion. He picks and chooses when he wants to be himself, I think. The owners drop by the store and admire his cleanly uniform appearance and level-headed attitude, and I share my conclusion that he's a competent team member but am not 100 percent positive if he's interested in ever associating with us once he decides to move on. When I came back from vacation, my concerns proved valid. He approached me in my office on the down-low. I questioned if he was willing to stay with the store and redact his two-week notice for more money, but he said, "I don't think so." I later discovered from other second-shift managers that he was displeased with the "tension, drama, and lack of promotion." He chose not to advise me of any of those complaints whatsoever, only alluding to some of them. Not entirely sure what about him confused me more: his passive-aggressive actions or his ability to subtly express wisdom to coworkers that even I had never thought of. Yeah, I don't know, man. Strange.

The whispers circling us are true. We talked it out and feelings were shared, always after hours in the night. Of all the guys who could have been enrolled in that class section and been assigned that specific seat, of course, it's him. Sitting beside me, I understand how he once felt about me. Right now, I cannot help but notice his distance and passiveness. He used to have stars in his eyes, but now he gives off a cold vibe that I'm so unfamiliar with. This man kills off every feeling. That's why girls who seek interest from him do not end up pursuing a committed relationship. A repetitive trend of emotion that he bottles and lets out unhealthily at his lowest always happened as we continued talking about what we "could have been." I'm totally convinced that's how he saw me from the start: for what I could have been to him. I could not begin to uncover his ways how I wanted because I could not uncover and sort out my feelings for him in enough time. Separate engagements conflicted more than we ever used to, but I wonder if he left that dance early because of me. Either way, as we drifted further apart, I thoughtfully messaged him to say I missed him, but it only seemed to aggravate him. He pushed and pulled until he decided to cut all ties with me, which hurt a lot, as you could imagine. From time to time, I reflect on those years with him in my life. Does he enjoy living this mysterious lifestyle? Like, who really is he? Was it just blind attraction for me? Did we miss out on something real? Accountability and forgiveness were on my mind, but he definitely grew conceited toward the end because I was left blocked out and ignored. I know that I'll probably never interact with him again. I've made peace with that, to be completely honest. I just thought we agreed to be friends—I guess he moved on to please himself. He never did have much to say.

As I draft a personal note on his exam, I question if he'll even pay it any mind. This is the second consecutive test I've administered in which he'd performed more poorly than he should have. He can do plenty better than a B plus. If he put forth the necessary effort, he'd realize that he is abandoning the pursuit of the very needs of Maslow's hierarchy that I'm presenting. My lectures alone are not enough to cause him to sleep every class. There's something else that's bothering him. He prefers to keep it hidden. When I look closely into the whites of his eyes, the window to his soul, I see struggle, and I'm worried he may not grasp that it could very well lead to his downfall. An energy drink sits atop his back corner desk, and I believe he tries his best to stay awake, but he's usually close to REM by my third presentation slide. His intellect is there, no doubt. He offers a stoic persona to the acquaintances he passes in my wing, but I can see through the holes in his facade. Always trying to be someone he's not, and that strains him. I know it. A few arms extended around friends and a few strangely specific visions he attempts to convey, but there will be no understanding. None. Not because he is incapable of captivating individuals, but because this lackadaisical, yet hardened, student does not lead a life remotely resembling the one he advertises. If all this was in his true nature, that'd be one thing, but there has to be a degree of nurture in his case, too. No way he befriends or associates with the socially powerful students without a reason. He knows of his dichotomous act, but I can only presume he's also aware that his deeply rooted compensations remain in the shadows. I'm willing to bet that in those shadows lurk an ugly truth through little fault of his own, but that fault line is proving finer with each sunset. What haunts him more than opening his eyes to see me returning a glance during class? Waking up. He must wake up. Before his life has been lived or gone about in an imprisoned-like manner. Do not enslave your mind, young man, it's not worth it. Trust me on that. I sincerely hope my notes and letters find him well and that he accepts them at face value. He carries a heavy burden with him. Perhaps his purpose in life originates from that burden. It would not surprise me.

Yeah, he—he's a different character all right. He always hooks us up with extra hot sauce packets and cinnamon starlight mints for our lockers. It's always hard not to exclude him because no matter what we say or bribe him with to spend a few nights with us, he rarely shows. That's why when he does come out, everybody goes crazy in disbelief that he's hanging with us. One thing I will say is that it seems like he's on two sides of the fence. Like he has to get permission from his own mind, somehow. We take his hat off and mess with his hair jokingly, but because he needs everything perfect, it sets him off. At some point, we're like, "Guy, just get over it, you know? Relax. Don't take everything so seriously." There was one time when we were having a dope weekend together, and all of a sudden, he got up and left because he had to go to the bathroom, even though I told him many times that we have two of them. Yeah, or the other time when he was adamant that I drive because he was paranoid that his truck would break down just five miles up the road. Above all else, why does he try so hard? Why does he put more effort into his appearance and outfit than making plans and having fun with us? Sometimes I converse with him, and he acts normal. Then there are times when he does not shut up. Then there are times when he looks nauseous from the thought of speaking to people, including me. My parents must think there's something wrong with him, too. I'll bring him back inside to have dinner after playing basketball and they're pleasantly surprised. They always express how nice of a young man he is and ask about him because they're curious. Curious for a good reason, because it's 2019, and they haven't seen me associate with this kid in like three years when we were just getting started. What do I even bother telling them about him? Not much more than I know: "He just has his priorities. He does things his way, whether we're with him or not." I really can't say if I'll ever see him again once we graduate. He's the type of guy to disappear. To leave and never return. None of my friends can figure him out, and we keep it that way intentionally now. None of my friends have had the chance to crack him emotionally. None of my friends have ever been invited to his house, even. He's generally a mysterious dude. Who knows him, honestly? He speaks and most listen. We'll be at the twelve-person lunch table, and he'll manage to have the entire far side of the cafeteria fussing over whether or not Uncrustable sandwiches have crust. He fends off many of our aggressive reasonings ridiculously as if he gets enjoyment out of bickering endlessly and trying new flows and cadences. Wait, now that I think about it, he did mention that his parents were divorced, and it was kind of messy. Could that be why he's like this? Ah, yeah, whatever. I don't know. Nobody here does.

Fixing his truck is never as straightforward as it should be, with the rust and everything. It does give us an opportunity to spend some time together, though. Now that we don't play ball as much, I rarely see him. Primarily, I'm concerned with where his girlfriend is, or if he even has one. It's always confusing because sometimes he acts like one of us older guys, then other times he adapts to what kids his age are doing. Then, he doesn't say a single word at family events that he organized and actively promoted. But if there's one thing I know, it's that he's going places. He sees us as valuable assets to his brand and expresses how crazy we are for not seeing the "inevitability of greatness" we'd experience if we collaborated in a family business. He drops by and explains some educational things to me, but never anything spiritual. When I ask him if there are any lady friends I should hear about, he always says "Nah, nah, not yet," as if he knows of the woman he'll end up with, including the exact time and place of meeting her, which he doesn't, obviously. We wish him a great, long life, but we're not sure if he fully understands what's meaningful and fulfilling in life and what isn't. I'm convinced he's set in his ways and would like to continue pursuing whatever it is that keeps him working so hard. I mean, he's just a bit different. He's always off on his own. If he's offered a drink, he doesn't eagerly accept it like a lot of adolescents. It's weird. His age relative to ours is convenient because we're able to bum him as our designated driver for all eight of us when brewery-hopping. Anyway, when his picture pops up on my phone, I'm ultimately left thinking of the scenes he had to witness at a young age and wondering if he lets that affect him the way it used to affect me. It's not easy to deal with, but here we are. Not much has been the same since then, and purely based on what he tells us, they'll never catch him.

Solitary Descent

For reasons unclear, besides nostalgia, I believe there is something so perfect about tranquil solitude in places you've spent lots of time. As long as I could remember, sitting in the basement enjoying video games by myself, hearing nothing but the buzz from the television and the air particles whizzing beside me, was encapsulating. Or the hours in the living room with nothing but the Wii Home Screen soundscape, the spinning of the ceiling fan, and the rattle from the fish tank to keep me staring off into space mesmerized in melancholy. Or the final private seconds in the old house when I looked back at the empty loft in which I experienced those kinds of moments before shutting the door that was once slammed to move out. Finding it strange that the least action-packed moments are the ones I relive most often, I continued on the journey to find clarity. Oh, and maybe some peace, as well.

Some distant place lodged in the grieving aftershock of Rick's passing, my mother, Rose, and I found ourselves heading toward the largest nearby shopping mall. Rose needed clothes and school supplies for kindergarten, and I simply wanted apparel that, in my eyes, was not totally lame and outdated. As my mother and I conversed, she twisted to disgruntledly advise me, "You sound just like your dad, you know that?" The vehicle's cabin went quiet, and my attitude drooped. This was most certainly not the first instance of hearing a phrase of that nature before, yet it aggravated me because it ruined my mood on an off day, temporarily. Drawing from what I've been told, again and again, it's the "big-headedness" I was supposedly adopting that she recognized. "Of course, I sound like him, he's my dad," I announced, slightly flustered. My mother was left shaking her head, and we continued on our shopping quest. Not three minutes later, I was the subject of fixing because she felt the need to lower my hand from my face while piloting the car. Subconsciously, I began chomping at my skin and nails like I had not eaten in days. An accurate scene to illustrate the trials of that time, yes, but not wholly. The things of this world I could not afford were the very things I desired most, and evidently, my mother was concerned I was living my life wrongly. Never going to be "the man" thinking like that, though.

Glancing up into the rearview mirror of my truck while driving to high school for the first day of junior year, I needed to be 100 percent positive that I was in the right gear and every last strand of hair on my head was in place precisely how it was conceptualized. Deciding to let it grow shaggy not to remain how I was, but to try and change my personal brand. Needless to say, pet hair on shirts and car seats is always a problem. Paying attention to the highway only now and again, I conducted final appearance evaluations. Hmm, let's see. Shades? Check. New shirt and pants? Check. New Jordan 1s? Yes, indeed. Downshifting to prepare for the traffic sign ahead, I settled into a devised persona of my creation. It was my desire to be more talkative, lively, and similar to the classmates I'd noticed were "normal" in their steady interactions and companionships. No longer an outlier, no longer weird, and no longer susceptible to emotional distress. Remembering that we need to be mentally bulletproof out here. Everybody knows the final years of school fly by, so I rapidly set my targets on all social variables that I could control to revamp what was dormant among the sea of people who knew nothing about me. Nothing of the sort.

The mentality and persona I uploaded in the truck worked its way into classes, as planned. Seeing the surprise in others' eyes as they witnessed me "come out of my shell" was intriguing, and it allowed me to monitor how well my adaptation was progressing interpersonally. In many lectures, I wanted to get everybody's attention and speak out of nowhere, so I did precisely that. Weeks that my social battery had run out of juice, well, those were abundant, too. A neglected, but mentionable quality of the devised persona was the "no longer caring" attitude. Getting what I needed from people and moving on was my approach. Furthermore, as it were, I gave out no clues to what I reasonably wanted from love. There were girls around whom I knew were attractive, sure, but opening up and introducing the real me was not something I was interested in nor comfortable with. If even you had not spent a lick of time with your true self, would you wish to allow an innocent partner to gaze upon it—whatever is there? Truly then they'd see—albeit only an eighth of the unframed picture—enough to draw their conclusions and shade in the rest for themselves. Because my mind was hardwired to overthink and focus heavily on worry, girls posed a threat to me mentally and I thought they were dangerous. Every subsequent connection I managed to spark, though, ended the same way: me leaving out of nowhere. "I said too much already" was the basis of my thought to depart. My favorite exit style was Irish, and I did not care what effect that posed on anybody, including myself.

As you know, socioeconomic rank and popularity were always on my mind, but when it came time to participate in the extracurriculars that defined popular people, I wanted no part of any of them. Not all that sure of what in the world

I was doing, I took much refuge at work. Upon the close of school days in which I exerted minimal effort, I'd restlessly race home to eat two, three, and sometimes four or five granola bars in my truck after changing into my uniform to arrive at work on time. Micromanaging every second outside of class became an integral part of my daily routine. It seemed a war had been waged, and that fighting led to odd damage being done physiologically. During an ordinary autumn Thursday-night shift, I slumped over a register counter in an absurd amount of sharp discomfort. My stomach was absolutely obliterated, or so I believed, because eating became more difficult by the day. This particular night was far worse than the other painful occasions of the gut damage. *Should I leave? Should I stay the last hour? It is fairly dead in here for a Thursday, so now's the best time*—were my logistic thoughts, and the mind-shattering neurotic thoughts reported my inadequacies sufficiently, as they do so well. Ultimately, I decided to interrupt the conversation my manager was having and asked if I could get out of there, and he had no issue with it. What proved to be the true hardship of that evening was the return home. Wondering why my stomach felt like a scrunched-up plastic soft-drink bottle and honestly thinking I may be on my way out of this universe somehow, for hours I lay awkwardly on the miniature sofa in my bedroom. Directly in front of me were the many homework assignments I'd been trying to stay away from, and at ground zero was the insurmountable stress finding ways to tighten its grip on me slowly.

If you've ever gotten your wisdom teeth surgically removed, or any other procedure, you understand the potential for mental anguish in the weeks following. Yes, when all the world's bustle now flows like molasses to you. The mind knows no such adaptation, however. It fancies working strenuously to take you places you do not need to be taken while recovering. The inadequacy rung on the ladder downward remained sturdy, so the force behind my pain-ridden eyes escorted me to that horrid destination. How could a seventeen-year-old possibly have an outlook on things this bleak? Great question. An unanswered one as I could not come to any conclusions while that night was spent in some type of agony. I'm sure you're familiar with that agony, too. I set out to understand why gastrointestinal issues were arising, and the most jarring variable was tangibly developing stress. I came to find out that the stomach usually gives warning signs about troubles in other areas relating to general health. Saving this lecture for the medical professionals, allow me to look both ways before taking yet another step down and thinking about all the ladder's hazards and inherent creaks for a moment in time.

Dark times one thinks of, eh? OK. In dark times, one wonders why they're pursuing even the things that are good for them and asks others if this is all some joke or riddle, an elaborate scheme, perhaps. In no sense outlandish, the ominous feelings originating in tension, drama, and confusion seemed to crawl back into life. Now that, I cannot conclude in yours. Slowly healing from my physical ailment, I returned often to the beginning of this recent lore. Interpersonal relationships at work flirted with the same type of arguments ingrained in my mind, and because I did not desire any part of the skirmish, I resorted to keeping my mouth shut to not put anything on the conversational chopping block. You know, hide behind the couch a little bit. Picking and choosing was not a social tactic I necessarily wanted to abuse, but the situations I was wrapped in warranted it. False promises or simply the change of managerial plans caused me to put in my two-week notice. So relatable and commonplace to us that it's not funny, but a joke was what I classified myself as in the elaborate scheme working against me. Although I left on interesting terms, I still time travel to the conversations with every friend I made there, and I trust you will not allow the face of amnesia to disarm you while dreaming of the past, either. Dream. Because when the day is done and our bodies are at rest, what do we have? A mind complex with unvisited memories. Here's to hoping the happenstances of tomorrow fit nicely beside the plethora of mind keepsakes of yesterday.

Oh, the pleasantries of secondary school. Sports, clubs, parking lot vehicular foolishness, and, in this case, a dance. Straightening out my glacier-white bow tie, I reflected on the past school dances and accepted that this would be one of the final events I'd make an appearance at. A voice in my head advised me to say, *Who needs these people? Go and do what you actually want on your own*, a penetrative soundwave I hushed because normalcy and hermits do not associate. Still, I hopped into my classmate's ride, and he too was anticipating a great night and was also dapper with a white bow tie. Grabbing as many pictures and appetizers as I pleased from the function before the dance, I felt alive, like

I truly belonged there. And rarely do large social gatherings bolster any sort of comfort mentally or emotionally on my end. Today was different, though. My attitude was worthy of experiencing a good time with the people I saw most, for a change. For the event, guys borrowed other people's tuner cars and the ladies provided them a reason to borrow other people's tuner cars. All else being the same, making people laugh was the best interaction I could give to another, and I was doing that charismatically. Simply flowing and loosening up.

Just a heady boy with his silly ambitions, I had a whopping conflict of interest at the dance. She was not two, but three people across from me while I busted out some atrocious dance moves. Expecting much more out of teenage fever and reaching the end of the road with this particular girl, thoughts sided with more potent feelings, and I decided to make my way to the doors and into the night like a phantom, without saying a word to friends, even abandoning late-night plans we made weeks in advance. The undisturbed walk back to my truck was something from a movie, with the rain falling torrentially and the emptiness of the side of the parking lot I stood in. If one positive came out of that evening, it was the grasping of the clear indication that a relationship was not on the table anymore. I was done trying with people, altogether. Frustration arose in the depths of mixed messages and pointless persistence. A third strike was swung on and missed and now, I knew the gaping difference between love and infatuation. I knew not to expect anything out of interest, even if what you extend makes you deserving.

Oh, yes. The spoils of youth and pleasantries are only fully relishable far beyond the origins.

Speaking of origins, the spoils of alone time were underway, which meant a handful of prizes could be claimed only if and when I managed to slide out of the tainting gossip with others and into the melodic visions and conversations with myself off the grid. The pace of life slowed dramatically, and for once, my mind's activity did, too. A period of much-needed nothingness was upon me. Robed, lounging in my reclining chair with a candle lit beside me, I relished in the knowledge of my unemployment, lack of commitment to friends, and the liberties my faith provided. A year stricken by death, tribulation, and lust I'd dreaded thinking about had finished, so plugging in to drown out the lacerating experiences with art forms like music and drawing took their place without spite. All the while, I understood that future greatness in ventures would surely occur, but didn't know how to apply the ideologies that propel respectable men forward or how to engage in masterful legacy living.

Who are we when those doors close, and those lights turn off at night? Who do we prove to be in the presence of only our minds, hearts, and souls? When no one is watching, personas differ from the group, we know. Night and day. But, for just a time, please, please let me take off this disguise and stop living someone else's life. Desiring many things, but not to sift through any more wreckage because of the voice, mask, and mystery the unpredictable vigilante caused. To update, my records indicate we may be on our way down even further. Without hope that this was all a brief dream or nightmare, I shook off my daydream in anatomy class and longed to be anywhere else, but preferably unbothered. In the wasted time, I pictured myself figuring out every mental impairment, or that they'd naturally drift away, but isolation would teach me what socializing could not: that the detriment finds its way back to you in the quiet through screams. Sometimes, the only place you wanted to be, perhaps a sort of mental utopia, is not as flawless as you envisioned. Far from it. Even while living with the shame and hurt of pivotal scenes on my conscience, in each instance when I reached places of solitude, I exhaled and thought in smug relief, *Alone—finally.*

Money Fever

Here we go again, I guess. It's frustrating when you have everything understood clearly and nobody else seems to grasp what it is that you're trying to communicate. You look away from them, growl, shake your head, and smirk as if to say, *I just wish they could see into my mind for a bit to see how it operates*. Bear with me through the upcoming clutter and metaphors, if you so desire. I suppose we will uncover the idiosyncrasies that light up brain scans abnormally and travel through the peculiar realities of obsession, even though running from those is ever so tempting short term.

These days, the most up-to-date and social people have immediate and almost limitless access to knowledge in their pockets, so this next think piece may not come as a surprise to you. Nevertheless, here goes: when men get their hearts broken, or are scorned or traumatized, they often become quiet. Strangely quiet. Not only in the sense of sound by mouthing words, but also locationally. Off the grid some of them go. Some of them become dangerous to themselves and others for better or for worse. Convinced the universe is out to get them and that rage is the only fundamental scheme needing to be balanced. Convinced that maybe life is not art, but a game, you know, not real. Retrospective realization is knocking me as I pencil this, but we'll delve into all these variables shortly, I promise.

"What kind of car is that?" asked my classmate Dexter as I scrolled and clicked through the websites of the finest vehicle manufacturers in honors language class on the school's laptop. "It's a V12 Bentley Flying Spur with a velvet and cream leather upholstered interior," I said, all uppity. Since we did not feel as though the lecture was going to benefit us in any way, Dex and I browsed the likes of Mercedes-Benz, Ferrari, and my other favorite brand, Porsche, to specify the expensive supercars we desired. It's difficult for me to imagine him feeling that these cars were attainable for us. As for me, I sat like a worm at my desk in the back of the class with my synthesis essay written and submitted thinking that there was no conceivable path in life that would not lead to me owning at least one or two of those stately automobiles. It just was not happening, in my mind. Of course, by now, you and I know the three cheeky words "in my mind" combined are hazardous, like playing with fire, almost. Without a flicker of concern about the potential danger caused by my mental complex because of the branched-out effects of the early 2010s, the continuance of a "larger than life" figure expanded.

When not inquiring about vehicles I had no business shopping for, my father and I played basketball at a local YMCA during my gap in employment. Even at age sixty-eight, he could still make three-point skyhooks look effortless and that never failed to amaze me or the other young guys in the gym. "Your grandpa's got game!" is what they'd constantly preach. Little did they know that he was my father. I never bothered to correct anybody about it because awkwardness presented a high probability of questioning and questioning left the door wide open for the truth, and thus, trouble. After a H-O-R-S-E shooting match that lasted for what felt like an eternity in the best way, we exited the court and talked about how neat it would be to golf down south somewhere before the 2020 spring golf season, if the world as we know it lasted that long. To play anywhere that was not ten degrees below zero and that neither of us had been before was ideal. Suddenly, a loud idea popped into my mind: *Arizona*. "Pops, let's go on a three-day golf trip near Scottsdale. I see a couple of teacher in-service days coming up in February." He was just as enthusiastic about the prospect as I was, and the flights were booked by sundown that day.

We are very competitive as it pertains to golf matches. From my standpoint, I learned everything I know about the game of golf from him, so you'd think I could beat him rather swiftly, right? Well, it is not that simple. This guy will be behind by three strokes with five holes to play, and he'll nonchalantly birdie a few, chip in once or twice from the sand traps, and hit the approach shots of his life while I stand beside the cart glancing between him and our scorecard, and like an idiot, think I still have a chance at winning the round. Wishing I had the magic touch on the course that he has, I drag raced a 1999 Dodge Viper from a red light on the way to dinner on the unsalted, ice-free streets. Strolling in slow motion through all the shopping malls in Tempe, my father and I just laughed. Laughed and enjoyed every luxury of the trip, but more importantly, our time together. Too often our shared time was lacerated by pain and depressing energies. This was much better, though. When the desert venture drew to a close and we were back treading snow and sleet, I reflected a little on my choices since obtaining my license and noticed a void amid the freedom of adolescence. Not sure if it was a fund void or a girl void, but hey, what harm could be done filling both?

Slouched on my father's sofa a week after our return from Arizona, I finished aloe-lathering my forearms, which were burned to a crisp and peeling uncontrollably from the desert ultraviolets and headed to a job orientation at a local grocery store. Figuring that the balance in my savings account was indeed the void, I was overeager toward compensation chasing, but it was made clear to me that scheduled hours came at a premium. Moreover, the desire for something unique for myself developed from witnessing Rick successfully carry out his side job of private laundry machine repair, and I thought that I might as well capitalize on my clean, control-freak nature and invest some time and energy toward a creative side hustle. That inspired creation was a small-scale vehicle interior detailing service that could supplement my lacking main gig. Around the time I intended to launch the opportunity to friends and family, though, an ominous cloud stormed into all our lives. That cloud was the coronavirus, and the very minute our high school announced that it was closing its doors for just two weeks, I speed-walked into the locker room to grab all my belongings because I had a strong inkling that the process would take longer than two weeks simply based on the weekly CNN Student News reports shown in American government class. Little did we know that was the last ordinary school day we'd experience for a few years and for some, forever. Since I was deemed an essential employee in the dreary era, I was fortunate enough to witness the roads to work vacate equally as much as the toilet paper and chemical aisles. On the bright side, I did not have to adjust to the six foot rule, because I'd already been distancing myself socially for years.

As luck would have it, a grocery store is an optimal place to make friends. I was in the right place because my mind advised me to cling to the future and dump the past, since junior year schooling was far from relevant. Having new friends around was perfect because it meant that they had no clue about my past, so I could freely select from a wide array of personas to use in conversations with them. The guys and gals I met while being a grocery clerk at that store are extraordinarily lovely people, most of whom are still in closer contact with me than others, but every morning, afternoon, and night and in seemingly every interaction, I remained consistent in only one thing: the facade. Cycling through my collection of cloth and disposable masks was something peers could see, but few souls, if any, ever knew I selected masked personas on the fly to remain under the radar and mysterious. The pandemic brought about a third side of me, one that even I did not know how to control, yet. The third side's refreshed powers included more versatility in conversing, money hunger, rage, vengeance-management skills, and revamped friendship separation improvisation. To be caught between friend groups would be the death of the multifaceted facade, and to be analyzed or tagged as mysterious became more of a self-worth and esteem-booster than to be loved and trusted. The fever.

Murky days turned into mystical nights slowly but surely, and many an evening angered me since girls I had feelings for rarely saw me the way I saw them. The inability to admit that my heart could lose was ever present, and I sunk comfortably into an even harder and colder exterior that adequately conveyed to girls that I was no longer interested in anything serious. Revenge was mine, now. More than willing to ghost anybody I had the slightest interest in if things did not have the envisioned path or trajectory. Many evenings in June were spent sleepless because controlling my blue feelings was impossible, not to mention the inescapable thoughts and memories prancing around in my hippocampus as if to openly mock me while tossing and turning. Unfortunately, even golf and weightlifting did not lift any burdens. Insanely, I remained hopeful that another repetition or another song or another paycheck would come along to spare the light of each day moving forward, but those worldly possessions were only of temporary fancy to my compromised amygdala calling all the shots.

The way our perceptions and actions can so rapidly switch and amplify—it's incredible to think that merely a single momentary interaction with a stranger could completely alter the trajectory of another's life plan and the things they value. Perspective is key, most certainly, but meanwhile, I was not interested in any of that "beautiful mind" chatter. The perspective I needed was my eyes watching my hands thumb through blue hundred-dollar bills and scrolling to see my bank account balance grow exponentially. I couldn't tell you the ages of my closest relatives, but I would have no trouble telling you the balance of my every account, down to the penny, at any given moment. No potential for requesting off work was available because I'd so quickly become addicted to working, getting cash, and holding on to that cash for dear life, hardly ever spending any of it. Additionally, there was an abysmal potential for attending family parties, mostly because I thought it was a lose-lose situation because I was not using the time to increase my savings or maintain my elusive being. With everything that took place and all that I chose to conceal, figuring that my actions were insignificant to the present-day circumstances seemed reasonably justifiable. With many absences and wordless appearances during summer behind me, I reluctantly prioritized preparation for my final year of high school. Heading back to school was anything but easy. The classmates I neglected to keep in touch with most of 2020's quarantine and I felt we could not possibly learn anything new senior year. So, my approach was to complete my schoolwork as fast as possible to graduate, get my hours in at the store to continue stacking cash, and hurry up to get a four-year chapter of my life called "college" started, one that I had to mentally prepare to endure because nothing sounded more like a prison to me than forced communication, intoxication, oblivion, added academic stress, and hunger. Perhaps the aspect of college that frightened me most was the thought of my supply of cash depleted for tuition payments and living expenses. Now that shook me to my core.

All that core-shaking would have been meaningless if no choice had been made as to where I'd attend university for business. I chose business because I love speaking with people if money is involved, and I also liked the idea of promoting and developing products and services into greatness. As I brushed road grime off a rear-door panel detailing for a customer, I decided to commit to a division-three university about two hours south of my hometown, because a role model of mine from prior years attended that business school and he seemed to have everything in perfect order, as I strived to have. Before any of us really knew it, fall was upon us, and few weekends could be escaped without seeing around five "Senior Sunday" posts on Instagram. That encouraged me, because it signaled the start of something new on the horizon for us as a class of 2021. I did not necessarily hate school, but I did not look forward to going most days. Scrounging enough dopamine to arise from the faint slumbers was increasingly tedious, and many of my successful classmates would likely attest to the same.

High school was stale, but my "Son-of-a-Baconator" burger sure was not. Man, I destroyed about twenty-five dollars' worth of Wendy's from a gift card in an adjacent parking lot like some kind of vulture. The car clock read 12:56 p.m. By the time I realized the time, I was already in drive and speeding down the highway, hoping to not be one minute tardy, knowing that could wipe out my psyche for days. Glancing at my speedometer, the needle accelerated almost as quickly as the worries in my head. Ninety, ninety-five the speedometer read as I swerved and cut off about three vehicles just to enter the off-ramp for the store's lot. Again, I jerked the wheel toward the parking stall, not caring about my surroundings or if I would cause a severe accident. In the moment I took off for the entrance, I could not seem to trust in the fact that I locked my door. So, there the mental predicament lay. Desperately needing to maintain perfect attendance while desperately needing to constantly recheck if my door was locked, even though I watched the metal lock go down and heard the locking noise sound seven times right before my eyes. Madness. Anyway, at 1:00:47 p.m., I rushed into work and clocked in with a certain type of swagger that only emerged because cash superiority reigned. All symptoms pointed directly to positive contraction of a mental disease known as "money fever," not COVID-19, and nothing could block the road to the pursuit of it, including scenarios difficult to admit like the latest OCD-ridden conundrum.

When you age gracefully to be old and gray, God willing, what life-defining moments will you look back on with deep pride and emotion? Are they the early mornings and late nights you chose to persevere through while studying for your degree? Are they the wasted times you spent with your love letting the strummed chords of life vibrate and flow to predict the outcome of that solo? Just wandering or wondering. Whatever they may be, take as much time as you feel to reminisce gracefully. Returning to reflect and think rightly, I believe that I'll look back on my money-fever days with the most emotion, not because I'm particularly happy about that era, but because of the wisdom I came out of it with. Currency and war was my life, back then. The chase for cash never seemed to end, yet it was all a blur. Marked by obsession and unresolved affliction, I would power through forty-five hour work weeks with demanding classes on my load, as well. Not wanting to let go of a single dollar of my "moldy money," as my mother called it, for anything, I paid tolls on my sleep schedule and body. Increased responsibilities at work and a highly set standard caused expectations for results to be at an all-time high, but I had descended to my all-time low. Too many shifts I would use my forearms as makeshift pillows for my skull while standing beside a cart to unload trying to muster a few minutes of shuteye. My dear friends at work would always approach and strongly advise me to take some time away from it all, but voices in the back of my head catered exclusively to my visions and what it would take to achieve them, so I never dared to lessen my load.

As if the mental and physical strains of life are not great enough, coming home to sit on the couch and watch television beside my family was not as ordinary as it sounds. The constant pressure of living up to the expectations I standardized in my head was debilitating but resting at my father's place gave my bones a chance to recover. Almost considering my mind a lost cause at this point, I began to loosen my behavior a bit around my family to relieve some pressure from the brain. After a short, peaceful drive back to our house that involved many melodic and conceptual music videos looping in my head, I had a conversation with Millie, who was back from college for winter break. I expressed some views and reasoning on my bitterness toward women, and she quickly countered by saying, "That's just your ego talking. Girls don't like that." All the while knowing she may have been on to something, I uttered, "It was a joke, my goodness," to downplay the hate within me. A molten rage had been building deep inside my chest since the start of the fever, and I was concerned secretly because of the susceptibility to self-destruct, like blowing up or physically fighting with someone because of the flames I'd been suppressing. Ridiculously, I'd even played foolish games with myself to encourage surrender to my ferocity. One of the games was based on a promise I made myself, one that included not allowing myself to get a haircut until the hot temper was undoubtedly eradicated. Months and seasons went by, and my hair appeared unsightly. The fever running its course.

Day by day, I further grasp and sympathize with some of the justifications held by those who are at their lowest and feel the need to partake in very potent, life-threatening drugs. Life is brutally difficult. There is no diluting that at all. Like, what are we to do with all the trauma and how are we to sort through the high heartbeat-per-minute totals as we recall past scenes? Run from them, I guess? Run until your demons respect you enough to leave you alone, I guess? Hide from all Holy Ghosts that try to lodge themselves between your dreams and your nightmares, I guess? Every soul for itself out here. Kill or be killed. You either take flight or assume a fight, I guess? There was no time for love then, so there's no time for vulnerability now, I guess?

Vertigo

We live in a performance-oriented society. The measures predominantly associated with success and status like grades, income, followers, connections, valuable possessions, and physique are paramount to outsiders looking into your life. So much so that you will inevitably be judged and even persecuted by individuals you may have never met before. Let's self-assess. Do you care about what other people think? As you were pushing your limits mentally and physically in whichever desired venture, did you ever stop and think that maybe, just maybe, you were unintentionally morphing into the human you thought you'd never associate with? OK, one more riddle for good measure: when life got so cold you thought frostbite would be your demise, did you beg for warmth or did you only long for a coat to carry on with? Strains from all directions enter and exit your brief existence, but your mind will never leave. Whether ordered or chaotic, it will be there to act as your best friend or worst enemy, quite like a marriage setup. It's the trust-required proximity in long-term relationships that presents the most risk but yields the most fruit.

The truth is that earthly existence is filled with unbelievably high highs and undeniably low lows. It can only be concluded that without them and the effects they both have on these campaigns that we say are different but are very much the same would be too uniform to matter. Elders refer to the little things in life as the unsung heroes, so in each dialogue you have between now and your hour of passing, remember that the influence and power you hold to instill in others can be remarkably abundant. Yet, we may clamor for weeks and linger in discomfort for who knows what reason because we underestimate the ability of the contraption ready and able to get you straightened amid many messes you find yourself in, which is the mind. The following question remains as we resume through troubled waters, and it's mighty important: Is your mind willing?

It's said that the more things change, the more they stay the same. In time, 2021 was set to be the grandest year of them all. Work, which meant money thirst would be quenched, graduation, which meant freedom, but not for long, because the start of my first college semester was four months out from that. Snug in between the earliest was the golf season that I'd been patiently waiting to play in. By this moment, obsession is potently evident, but the sound of competing in a sport that is make or break based on personal performance was music to my ears. It was all I could think about at school and work. While waiting, I tossed back and forth the brutally upfront question, *When will I start living?* every day from New Year's to the Ides of March. I learned the reason behind why we are to beware it the hard way.

The moment the clock struck 9:00 p.m., I was clocked out and halfway into the pressurized exhale I traditionally released while relaxing in my car after work. So drained that thinking straight was in no way possible, alongside the hope of not having to live through the lulls of depression, I sluggishly plugged in my phone to my cassette-to-aux adapter for music. The drive from the store to our place was twenty-two minutes, and I had just the extended play to fit the foggy night's atmosphere. Once settled and cruising, I began to drift off to sleep as if it was a lecture nap and had to jerk the wheel left to stay on the road. These conditions were in place five nights a week, and given the circumstances, I'm lucky to have made it wreck free those years. Towing every bit of stress, worries, and melancholy into the kitchen with me once I got home, I immediately raided the fridge and pantry in search of enough grub to satisfy my hankerings for another twelve hours and to recuperate all the calories missed the previous eight. Upon finishing the last bowl of an entire family-size Fruity Pebbles box, I felt my mother's presence as she flipped the light switch to chat. "How was work?" she asked. "Same old," I mumbled disinterestedly in low alto. Letting down my cracked, bloody hands from my bag-ridden face, I finally gave into the forces of life and opened up about my struggles with depression, primarily. "I mean, I just can't seem to get out of this feeling. I've been stuck for such a long time, like, when am I going to start living? I'm just way too young to be feeling this old." Alongside other addressed topics, she suggested trying to talk to a professional in therapy to release all that was on my mind. Every occurrence of the "therapy talk" took place at night because that's when I'd be down to my lowest with caught-up demons. Never completely against her proposal, I'd always remark that calling for psychiatric assistance in the morning would be the most appropriate move to make. Those mornings were always of the opposite wave, though. Attempting to shed a tear at night would most certainly cause me to wake up feeling like a million bucks in my conceits. Like, *Nah. Nah. There wasn't any way I was about to spend my time and money at therapy, man. I don't need any of that nonsense.* Some may ask why a charismatic high-honor roll kid would feel this way regarding his situation during the light of day considering everything he felt by nightfall. To that, I would only respond with the same reason everybody boasted and claimed that the Titanic was unsinkable.

No drama. Please let these words be everything but shallow to you. And a foretaste of the succeeding phase. These are the circumstances great people can find themselves entrapped in. Perhaps the most fearful we've been as a people is the initial knowledge of life's duality and its difficult art that some call living and some call nothing because they've never caught a glimpse of the natural excellence that the masses should strive for: balance. To be missed, to have your absence felt. If you and I are not living, active beacons of truthful light for others, then what's the point of all this? But we all carry intrinsic worth, meaning, and existential purpose. Against immense odds that you would not even exist, you've been granted life and it's real, very real. The choices you make have compounding entanglements. It is challenging to compartmentalize fear and intelligence in times of tenderness but believe there is hope. Have full faith that you can make it out of your detriment. Know that I sure do. If you have had the enlightened moments of every significant emotion, experience, and memory come full circle, relish in it. Take necessary and appropriate action for yourself and your loved ones guided by God and the rest may simply take care of itself.

Nearly as blind to the above ramblings, I could not have seen what came next for anything. Around a month following the kitchen nightmare, my father and I were headed back to his place after church, as we'd been attending regularly for five or so years. On the way, he and I settled on a drive-through to target our cravings and while we waited for our food in the car, I noticed a certain tingly, claustrophobic, and twitchy reaction coming from somewhere. I did not know the source. My mind started to race and behind the sunglasses, I was hyperventilating. Never in my life have I experienced an anxiety attack straight from the textbook quite like this. I had not the slightest clue what to do or say because I was with someone, and I did not want to cause any stressful situations. Striving to be alone as quickly as possible because of the wrecking ball of forces colliding, I tried to manage my breathing, but was unsuccessful as overthinking crowded logic as a feeling of this magnitude had not been felt before. Was this the unavoidable self-destruction that I knew about or was this iceberg avoidable? Without sufficient answers to those concerns, I nonchalantly requested that my father drop me off by my car to be alone and figure out what on earth just transpired.

Once I was home and a tad more relaxed an hour later,

my mother, Rose, and I spontaneously decided to go on a hike since it was a gorgeous day. I chose to leave them in the dark about the seemingly insurmountable anxiety and depression because it was light outside. Wondering why I only felt this "off" on Sundays, I snapped some pictures with those closest to me and asked Theresa if she would take a quick photo of me on the park's wooden steps. The picture turned out satisfactory, so it was consciously posted on Instagram with the caption: "Making my way up, but Sundays I rest." That was true in a sense, but Sundays were the only day in the week in which I was not making money, so I was not going up and certainly not resting with all the stressors killing me from the inside. All was well with the world, however, because all they saw was a shaded smirk and a clever caption in nature with no indication of distress or worry about one thing present. With the golf season and school beginning to sizzle, I resumed full control and composure to try and prevent any further funny business from happening again.

As we slash through our days, we draw parallels between certain unrelated things that we've experienced and downgrade them. For example, I reflect on all the short putts that should never be missed and how I regularly missed them. Then, like many others, relate that to how ridiculous some of the problems we used to have were in times of regret. Because how is one to succeed in the big picture of life while failing to hit the mark in the simplest of practices? To translate, I missed many makeable putts, and the beginning of the end was upon our class of 2021.

On this day we became legendary, but while I sat in

a folding chair among many of my classmates I came up alongside during the graduation ceremony, my aura was emotionless. Shaking me out of a trance-like daydream, an outstanding classmate spoke about the infamous discussions we had in our research writing course to the crowd. Because I had no care then and noticed a quickly expanding mental rift between me and my peers, I felt strangely obligated to give conceptual, but impromptu presentations to our class of four and enjoyed conversing deeply with them about life and its unpredictable ways. History does repeat itself if you let it. Like the lunch table monologues and debates, the aforementioned discussions must have left a memorable impression on people, which was interesting to know. As the daydream vanished, I hoped he would not go any deeper with the story to remain elusive, but admittedly, a small part of me wished for a more substantial slice of the attention pie. The special day we all envisioned for so long was coming to an end and it rarely ever is what you believed it to be. That's simply the trap of desiring a thousand different things at once. As soon as you accomplish or obtain one thing, you're on to the next objective without any plunder of content in your appreciative pockets.

On a brighter note, I had made it to sectionals golf at the end of the season by barely playing well enough at regionals. Taking off work to play a practice round the day before the event, I was relaxed and ready as I shot my career-best score and wished for that same positive energy to radiate into the meaningful round. Flushing iron shot after iron shot warming up, I felt balanced and flowed naturally as my father watched from behind. The knowledge that I was making him proud kept me in good spirits as we walked toward the first tee. Recovering adequately on the first few holes, I still folded and missed makeable four-footers, and rage began to boil inside. Some fellow teammates made the trip to watch me play, so I wanted to give them something, anything to rave about. Spanning holes five to fifteen, though, my mind raced uncontrollably about everything under that sweltering sun, including the money I was missing out on by playing in the tournament. Around hole sixteen, the odds of saving the round were abysmal and shame came down heavy, like the way I hit my approach shots. In complete disbelief that the last round of competitive school golf I played resulted in such a disastrous way, I tapped the ball in on the eighteenth green and hoped for a miracle to get into the state round as an individual entry. Sipping some ice water on the clubhouse balcony, I felt a fierce anger toward myself and knew that I let down the people who believed in a future of golf greatness. Results were released later, and state proved to be only a wish as my lackluster round was three strokes too high.

We conceal truths all the time, don't we? The reasons behind our disguises are left unknown to the vast majority around us. I'd been offered to play golf collegiately for a strong program but considering my sporting peril history and lack of mental stability through obsessive-compulsiveness, I politely declined the opportunity to save myself and others the shame. So now that it was a full-go for the preparatory summer leading to the abyss-like entrance into college, one last major push for money was to be made to dodge debt like a matrix. Three short vacations were planned with family to spread throughout the season, and relaxation was the prize awaiting possession.

Splitting grocery loads and unloading pallets of upscale dog food sounds straightforward enough, but my brain took the work and tangled it in whichever direction it pleased. Feeling like I was on the verge of exploding and checking into a psych ward while getting through a usual Tuesday, I declined the break my manager advised me to take in fear of losing my flow. Daily acts like sitting and chatting with peers became labor intensive because managing the Tourette's-like motions many people say I make was unfeasible. A sudden shake seen by a coworker meant I was gone, but even for the over shameful, shame decreases enough to provide a pathway for the visibility of a plethora of disorders. No time was more evident than when I threw a fit and argued with my financial adviser regarding the potential loss of savings from the effects of the borderline economic recession, as if it was some Ponzi scheme against me. Or when on vacation with my brothers, sisters, nieces, and nephews whom I only saw three or four times a year, and all I could think of were cash levels and outside perceptions. Disguised as an orderly chap on the outside, but on the inside, it had to have looked like a tornado went through. Some drown mental anguish with alcohol. However, I had no interest in that as it only amplified mental anguish later. My mother must have thought I was crazy with how noticeably anxious my disposition, or facade, was reduced to. Riding the waves on the boat on a picture-perfect evening with loved ones was thwarted because of much greed and covetous thought. Dizzying reality.

Riding that same wave, my father had booked a round for us to play at an exclusive links golf course as a retirement present to himself and me. He'd been eagerly waiting to play it with me all spring, so I tried my best to improve my game to not appear a fool out there. Alas, allowing corrupt financial distress and lack of par-level play fog the gorgeous sights of the waterside course took precedence over spending quality time with him. Dizzying reality featuring hideous truths.

"It's our time now, we'll see what we do with it," was the caption of another Instagram post I made during the next vacation with my father. This time, we went to the Field of Dreams. The reasoning behind the wordage was to accurately represent the current position our year's class found themselves in. When society releases you like a butterfly out of a chrysalis, you're left speechless because you cannot believe that this amount of freedom has been slid over to you. It's yours and it appears that it's here to stay. Are you free or shackled by the tricks your mind plays on you? We shall see, as the latter half of the caption was meant to convey a sense of uncertainty and gainful opportunity. Never speaking in Morse code, as it may appear on the surface, a little thought, context, and perspective must be placed on it to decipher, though. Another vacation in the books and another wasted chance to revive a lost mind in the memory vault. Let's spin it to unlock and gaze upon the next one.

This entire memory museum revolves around the calendar, and your eyes have landed upon early August, the final month and final relaxing vacation opportunity before venturing off to university living. Theresa, Rose, and I arrived at a cabin where we resided for three days "up north," and I thought about how flustered I probably made my manager after reluctantly requesting off for a third time that summer. The next morning, I poured some cereal into a foam bowl and looked out the window at the wooded tree canopy beside the tranquil waters. Finally satisfied after three bowls' worth, I stood up, and in doing so, felt a strange dizzying sensation. Stunned by it, I lay down for a minute to restabilize the world because it was spinning approximately eight-seven miles per hour counterclockwise. Little did I know that minute would morph into an hour, and then five hours, and by sunset, I was still in the same position because moving meant vomiting and loads of anxiety. As my mother and Rose returned from their day's adventure, I was on my back with my eyes fully closed, believing this was going to be the end, that death was imminent. Their concerns for me were wrapped in thoughts that it was an exotic disease, but echoes of vertigo flooded my consciousness as I'd heard of the unbalanced spinning episodes and feared them. Surely no exotic disease had been contracted, intoxication was not a factor, and I felt normal hours before the incident. Perhaps it was stress induced. Perhaps it was the stress of accepting that I was becoming the very man I always told myself I would not be. The stresses of everything outlined thus far engaged in thermonuclear fusion with one another to produce a series of bizarre anxiety attacks in several forms. Mhmm. Yes. That seemed more accurate. After around twenty-five hours of bedridden peril, I carefully arose and tried not to tilt my head too quickly, because we had to hit the road for our home at sunrise. Thankfully, the spinning sensation decreased enough for me to function, and we packed our belongings.

Armed with the strength to disarm calmness and arm debilitating sickness, I grew more uneasy and longed for reassurance that I was not going to suddenly disintegrate because of a simple assignment or something at school. Still, I chose not to mention any of this to a physician or mental health professional, thinking that if I tried to seek help, I would not know where to begin, or if they would even believe the actual, raw concepts occupying my mind and the recollections flowing from my lips. So, we can say that staring at the face of adversity is not an enviable task. The traumas that plague you and me will reappear like the dewfall on morning grass if we avoid taking action. An all-new chapter of our lives, as well as this reflective manuscript, is approaching briskly. Cheers to knowing that we're one day closer to achieving cerebral freeness together despite our distance.

Prisoner

Fitting in. Keeping it cool, calm, and collected. Clamoring the correct, trendy phrases to be seen as a chill person and accelerate the increase in positive perceptions about yourself. Altering your behavior if people you find attractive are around. Disregarding outsiders' claims that you have a good head on your shoulders because you know what really lies beneath the surface. Engaging in activities you definitely would not normally engage in to earn the respect, or lack thereof, of individuals you do not know or wish to know. Sabotaging and molting from the persona you may have created or simply been up to this point. Overthinking the overthinking that you're overthinking. Reminding yourself that others are actually normal and will not react to things in the manner you envisioned abnormally. Being nervous over situations yet to occur and over the effects inflicted on you if you would mess up or get compromised. Trusting nobody. Failing, ha ha. If you ever have. Joking about a character that is just like you to friends while abusing cheap food and drink. Partying and having a dance with all the wrong intentions. Delving further into your tool bag of sociological tricks to remain safe physically and avoid an unfortunate end to this life we all endure. Long suffering countless issues and suppressing intrusive thoughts to keep your flow going for as long as humanly possible. Returning home from all the terror and fun with your back shaped like a question mark. Wishing upon stars. Breathing heavily and learning how to breathe, because let's face it, the unsettling nature of apprehension caused by what you've chosen to be is beyond frightening. Running so fast and so hard you find that shin splints are far from your greatest concern. Praying for a way out of your disturbed self. Battling amnesia. Looking up with your neck bent out of shape to see gloomy skies showcase suspended water droplets. Thinking. Scheming. Plotting deliberately month after month and year after year. Going crazy wondering if this is all worth it and if you're the joke among normalcy or not. Yeah—if anybody knows, well, you know.

When you ask a former postsecondary-school student what it was like to live out a stereotypical college kid lifestyle for years, they'll probably hit you with a raunchy anecdote or two, chuckle, then gaze away smirking in slight disgust with themselves because they recall some of the darkness encompassing the educational resort and the variables within it. Recall what was stated about nostalgia earlier. It's bluesy for a reason. Four, evidently five times you have explored distinct darkness realms in this vice-ridden phase, but this one appears progressively daunting. All good things must come to an end, at least here on earth, as they say. A transition or shift in the brain's foundation could very well be on the horizon for us as it's always darkest just before dawn. Unfortunately for me, the dormitory room window faced the opposite direction, so a shift was not discernible.

The hour had come to unpack my three totes and four plastic bags of personal items into the fourth-floor dormitory room, or prison cell, that I had never been in before. Per usual, Theresa and Rose were alongside me, and the boiling late August day had gotten the best of me. Having exerted most of my energy carrying my wardrobe and technology up four flights of stairs, no energy remained for serenity with them. I was overcome with anger as I thought Rose was being annoying, and sticky laundry detergent was in the school's malfunctioning dresser. Not to mention, my video game cases and books were not perfectly aligned and in alphabetical order yet. As if the short-tempered ticking time bomb exploded, I threw my hands up in the air and gave up trying to appease OCD, because Rose had an important meeting for school to attend later that day, and we were in somewhat of a rush. Enraged that scenes of this nature were still transpiring often, especially following the scary spin-cycle adventure weeks earlier, I looked forward to beginning classes even less.

"Fake it 'til you make it!" That's what they tell you. Well, we had made it to college, so we might as well continue faking it, you know. My newest acquaintance, my roommate, Kendrick, and I spent the days leading up to the start of the semester together by wasting away and trying to consciously figure each other out discreetly, as it can be strange adjusting to living with an all-new person. He hailed from a more densely populated, affluent city versus my rural village origins, which created an atypical blend of preconceived notions. No wonder, he must have been thinking that I was an interesting character because of the unparalleled neatness of my side of the room, cleverly supplied with a hand vacuum I used to collect salt and debris from neighbors regularly and painstakingly. Coming with university living were the refreshing opportunities to be laughed at and to laugh at yourself for the ridiculousness of your daily habits. Swiftly, I became known as "the guy with the hand vacuum we borrow occasionally to clean up dropped lettuce." For the first time, everybody's weaknesses were on display equally as much as their strengths, so my glaringly obvious OCD and moderate antisocial ways projected to people who had preliminarily judged me strictly based on how I organized, carried myself, dressed, and combed my hair—which was trim, because I cheated in my contest and got a haircut. Not to fool anyone, my rage was most certainly not eradicated.

Parading around the rural campus as ignorant dudes, Kendrick and I were exploring all that the university had to offer. Surprisingly, we looked at each other in disbelief that we'd been attending for a week and had already experienced 90 percent of what the school offered. Walking around aimlessly and blasting music became the norm, as far as time passing was concerned. Contrary to our current memories and beliefs, those are not the only activities we took part in.

Classes had begun, and I was five books deep into *Meditations* by Marcus Aurelius, a stoic assigned reading in our writing skills course. Admittedly, the only reason I entertained the thought of reading it was because our professor maintained my undivided attention in class, and I thoroughly enjoyed listening to his lectures. Besides the gospel, it was the first glimpse of wisdom literature I'd been exposed to, and it made me look upon most things differently, especially nature and the nature of people, in general. The sun set earlier and earlier, and alongside the fallen leaves came a completed rhetorical analysis essay outlining rhetoric used by Aurelius, obviously, as well as the parallels between the assigned reading and the Book of Proverbs, since I recognized the construct from my father's drowsy basement nights. Writing was never a chore once I was flowing, and I finally had freedom to write the paper I wanted to write while still conveying an appropriate, cohesive message. Thoughts of "maybe college isn't that bad after all" converted to authentic positive words to Kendrick, who by this time knew far too much about me for comfort because, like the pandemic, there was no way I could go maskless for long without being spotted acting fraudulently.

Speaking of comfort, my closest confidants and I tried our best to endeavor beyond acclimation, but Kendrick was expressing extreme displeasure with the university and wanted to transfer a month or two into our first semester. Initially, I thought he was making obnoxiously grim claims and needed to lighten up immediately, but after a couple of weeks of noticing nearly all of the student body wasting no time in packing up and leaving on Thursdays around noon, I began to share similar frustrations.

Concealing my internal problems was rudimentary because years of experience were solidified, and I never complained about them because, well, nobody cares. That's just the way it is. I found rather jarringly that problems were not as natural for others to cover up, however. Due to the five-foot gap between our beds, it was clear that I was not alone in the constant struggle with depression. You see, Kendrick and I were tormented by aligned feelings of blues and discouraging hopelessness, but the reasons and fundamental coping mechanisms we utilized could not have differed more. Many of us realize true friendship flourishes while bonding and fretting over similar pains transparently, and I believe that's precisely what occurred with Kendrick and me. As the semester aged, my despairing and tainted outlook on life surrounded by wisecracks to balance out others' complaints about college life boiled down to chats that sounded like a complete album through it all. A common pessimistic dialogue snippet exalted directly from our lowest during a time-wasting stroll in a vacant campus lurks here.

A Conversation with Kendrick

Kendrick: "And I just want more for myself. I'm headed back to work. Managed to scrounge three shifts this weekend. There's just nothing to do here!"

shared chuckles

Milo: "Yeah. I haven't seen my family in months, either, and when I do see them, I'm never present—you know, never in the moment or comfortable. Once anxiety came in this year, it pretty much took over, not gonna lie."

Kendrick: "Yeah, you twitch and shake all the time, too, man. For me, it's been the gloominess. Not wanting to do any homework or study and I'm not even burned out. That's why I go downstairs to the music room at around eleven every night to work. During the day, I can't focus. But you're never awake after ten, or nine o'clock for that matter, so it doesn't affect you at all."

Milo: "Aye, at least I don't procrastinate. Kind of hard to do that when your mind forces you to slave away at whatever it's obsessed over or self-destruct. I mean, there are times when I'll be running late because I brushed my teeth for five minutes 'cause I can't miss a spot, and because of that, drive recklessly to make it on time. Based on that kind of thing, my OCD is so bad it could end up killing me if I'm in the wrong situation. It sounds wild, but, like, seriously. That's my problem, and it's getting worse. I'm a prisoner to it now. Same with how I've been feeling about girls, man. The last thing they are interested in around here is reality, and then they go and complain that no one wants them."

Kendrick: *sighs* "Yeah. It's getting ridiculous, but I also think you should get out there again. The right girl is out there for you, bro. But yeah, I'm starting to not care enough to try with 'em anymore either. I've been played twice already this year."

Milo: "No doubt. I thought y'all had something genuine going on. Guess one of her friends brainwashed her. That's how it goes every time. All they do is chatter. If you aren't chill with her friends, you aren't going to have it last. Unless she actually loves you. In that case, there you go."

Kendrick: "That's facts. Every day I come back from class and I'm just like "What are we even doing here, man?" This is all some joke. They say youth is wasted on the young, but here we are wasting away our wasted youth and we're not even stupid."

Milo: "Agreed. What kind of nineteen-year-old besides me goes to bed at eight o'clock sharp, has a Mr. Coffee machine on his nightstand, drinks his coffee black, and cleans his room weekly? Who do you know? Just me, I know. If I wasn't an outcast to everybody else, I wouldn't be nineteen going on seventy-five, dawg."

Kendrick: "Ha ha. That's actually crazy. It's also crazy how you've never actually touched the ground 'cause you always wear slides in the room. No shame in it, though. You do you. As for me, I'm usually lying in bed with my

Beats on with the volume cranked, wondering where it all went wrong, so terribly wrong."

Milo: "Well, for starters, you chose to live with me. *laughs* But if I had the answer to that question, man, I woulda been fixed a long time ago. Long before vertigo or even the depression that only like two people know about."

Kendrick: "Yikes. This is all a simulation with depression hitting me like a freight train."

Milo: "What's sad is that this is real. This is our current reality. But nobody, and I mean nobody you care about liking you cares about how you feel or what you're up to in your free time. Why do you think I've been focusing on myself so much? People are only interested in whatever little thing they can use you for. Remember that. Oh, and you're too nice. I don't want to see you getting played anymore, all right?"

Kendrick: "I'm not down bad enough quite yet to start taking social advice from you. I've seen you talk to like three girls here who you already knew. If I am, I'll let you know."

Milo: "Ha. Fair enough, guy. *opens grading app* Wait, bro, are you serious? Why did I get four points off on this?"

Kendrick: "Bruh. A 96 percent and you're angry. Take it."

Milo: "Nah. Rather leave it. Like the past."

Real friends wish to see you grow, learn, and succeed. They wish to hear you laugh until your ribs hurt and hear the song your soul sings. They wish to notice your mind at ease, not over contemplating. If you've ever been the subject of fixing, maybe even in some sort of intervention-style environment, you know exactly what it's like to understand that the life you live is not understood. It can be extremely irritating to realize and mentally grasp that you're the enigma everybody wishes to dissect and use for entertainment, even. Figuratively, an empty room with no light on: depression. Literally, an individual imprisoned but at war with himself as he witnesses several acquaintances stare into him as if to decrypt his secrets. Of course, conveying your metaphors is never easy, because if people do not understand you, how could they possibly reason with the abstract, yet meticulously chosen topics you speak of? Face it. Your behavior lends itself to the dangerous camel-like extremes of bottling and bursting emotions. Those are the components and surroundings of a captive mind. Blessing or curse, vice or not, we shall see, eventually. But right now, it seems as though the intervention connotation is not bolstering the argument that it is not a vice.

In fearful avoidance of everything that was wrong with my antics, alongside friends Kendrick, James, and Benny, I was shown through enlightening experiences that staying inside my head and social shell was not going to fix me. Nonetheless, I would always revert to my usual, highly unusual, ordered behavior of control seeking, worrying enough for a small village, and being in bed by eight o'clock every night because my schoolwork was finished and nothing besides emptiness and a feeling of not belonging accompanied any other activity besides sleeping. Feeling empty and completely uninspired in a room so crowded you can hardly move. Yes. You and I know that feeling all too well. The adaptation to college life seemed to have occurred completely, as well as the adaptation to anxiety's gifts to the facade, which had increased its superpowers one last time. Including existing features along with newly developed craftiness in social interactions involving persuasion, instantaneous lie cross-referencing capabilities, and innovative decision-making techniques, I lacquered a mental construct expanding over the course of three phases. Although heading into 2022 lost in most integral spaces, my final hurdle in the race to recency, anxiety, had offered nonchalant strengths that previous facade versions had been missing dearly. At the time, it was a much-welcomed surprise.

We're witnessing history at this very moment, whether we want to acknowledge it or not. The history of mind morphing. Unforeseen threats were being posed to the facade because an old soul simply does not fit the description of an ordinary and irreverent college kid. With that, I was to appear as a threat on the exterior. While the cold look worked in my favor for most of the school year, the topic of transferring to a different university arose again. Only this time, the move was proposed by James and Benny, and it was Kendrick who was undecided about whether he wanted to leave, so he waited to make a decision. Kendrick and I had become close-knit allies. I considered him to be a brother. Never in my life had I actually gotten close enough to another person my age to be referred to as a true best friend, but I concluded that he and I are in fact best friends. Which is why deciding to transfer universities was so emotionally strenuous. The type of emotions I tried my best to avoid, but here is where the connections were, and here the emotions were. Steaming hot problems between me and dear friends came about, and in an attempt to extinguish them before an inferno, I asked my dawgs who were staying at the university to be a part of my family because I desired not one more faded friendship. Determining that I'd do everything in my power to ensure that there would be no more stray dawgs. Meanwhile, a disconnect between Kendrick and me arose conversationally, and all I could manage was looking out the window. As strange as that sounds, the second half of freshman year was spent looking out of our fourth-floor window. Sometimes for a few seconds, for a few moments, and on weekends, I'd catch myself gazing out our window at the sixty-foot-tall tree and the road everybody took to "get outta dodge" for a few hours at a time. With no car and nothing better to do than read Bible scriptures, I counted cars passing by and neurotically reviewed my past and present iniquities while guilt seeped in. Ironically, the prisoner of my compulsive tendencies that appeared successful and oddly fair on the outside was very much living like an inmate on the inside.

The majestic hill I forced Kendrick to stare at with me out of our window was finally cleansed of all mud and winter-littered cigarette boxes, so I grabbed the football under my ornately made twin XL bed and rallied the dawgs to toss the pigskin. We were wheezing and panting from lack of oxygen and lack of being in halfway decent shape just five minutes in, but that did not stop us from looking back at the residence hall towers and promising ourselves to make the most of our final weeks around campus. If we were not studying haphazardly or out to the gym, James, Benny, and I were usually destroying any and all food available like usual, ravenous young guys. On a mellow Wednesday evening with two weeks remaining in our second semester, steak quesadillas were being served at the dining hall, so you know that we were there. I voraciously finished my plate of side vegetables and out of nowhere, started spewing a monologue about thinking inwardly, or reflecting, to become better people. James and Benny essentially looked at me like they were thinking, *What possessed him to randomly say all that?* Through the undeniable characteristics of that enlightened talk, we eventually spoke authentically without clamor and without concern and shared intimate details about our lives growing up and our lives at the moment, which revolved around divorce and its branching consequences. There was no chance that bonds between us would have grown if I had not brought about thinking inwardly on a whim. That initial result encouraged me. Maybe cerebral comfort and calmness were possible. Wishful thinking, probably. Like, is any thinking of mine done rightly? Confusion lingered in the general vicinity of the annual spring and summertime blues that depression brought forth. Now that the expensive facade was fully upgraded and implemented into daily practice, taming it consciously within conflicting psychological brainwaves sparked feverish dialogues like this to unfold regularly.

An Overstimulated Mental Conversation

Cerebrum: "Hold on, hold on, hold on. Wait a minute, that monologue connection relieved a significant amount of your overstimulated activity, so let's pursue more of that mindfulness and pray and meditate more often, too."

Amygdala: "Overstimulation?! You cannot be serious, my guy. I've had to fend off facade threats and outside rumors from all angles and keep tabs on the cleanliness of the room. How do you reasonably assume I can just magically start healing now? I'd say I'm overworked!"

Cerebrum: "I'm not at all saying that the facade system we've been using hasn't gotten us way further than otherwise possible, but it's definitely time to start compromising, and that begins with your responsibilities. You're limiting him now. Stop holding him captive. Here, take a look at my records. His cortisol levels are quite literally off the charts perpetually. We cannot remain at these release outputs for much longer."

Amygdala: "After all these years of development? Unbelievable. It's almost irreconcilable, and I wash my hands of this nonsense! You'll probably turn his eyes blind to all of this, too. Like you had with the whole *thinking inwardly* conversation. See how that one worked out? How many years of private intelligence have we lost over your compromise? I'll work him into the ground this summer if I feel like it. I don't care. What's crazy is that he'll probably get through it because I have him so ordered. You cannot be trusted with leading operations anymore after claiming he's what? A prisoner? I'm the one force that can get him out of this mess, and I fully intend to. Notice how everything he has is because of me and this rage I instilled in him. Get a grip on reality."

Hippocampus: "Yeah, if I could get a word in, thanks. Allow me to fight the amnesia you caused. I'll have you know that the corrupt money hunger, obliterated vacations, oh, and the vertigo episode triggered by your cowardly self has yet to yield any health improvements in here. Back me up on this."

Cerebrum: "I agree. 100 percent. If we don't steer him in the right direction and make necessary changes, then you're going to kill him. You're going to be the reason his worldly exit is painfully bewildering to his friends and family. Your sins will not be on me much longer as we will not exist anymore because of you. I haven't even introduced him to his soul yet, man. It's right here! It's been right here all along! *grunts* Let him take—"

Amygdala: "*Enough*! Enough! Look at his life. Look at his image. Look at his reputation. Look at his trajectory. *sighs* Guess we'll have to throw those out the window, too. Same way as the looks you made him stare to think about life positively or whatever silly little lies you two tell yourself on the daily. Nothing nice out here, guys. Except what could become of him if you let me continue doing my job and maintain progress toward where he needs to be. Let's get on the same page here."

Cerebrum: "You should be ashamed of yourself. Oh, wait, you are!"

Hippocampus: "All these memories I oversee, and not one of them disproves my theory that history repeats itself. Seriously. Do something about this."
Amygdala: *exhales and grunts angrily*

Sweet Father Time brought May 12, 2022, a bittersweet moment for a relatively bitter student. With the dorm room looking the part of a despaired cell, with nothing on the white-painted brick walls and the dark blue mattress pad I had not seen since moving in, the day had come to take my final exam and ship out with a fourth of college completed. Thinking negatively like, *Ugh. Only a fourth,* as I slouched in the lounge chair of our vacated residence hall, it was easily noticeable that everybody already left the premises. They, too, probably wanted nothing more than to go home. Just me and my vices alone together again. Gently closing my laptop upon completing the test, I looked to my left and drank the all-encompassing feeling in. Here it was, an empty room in which I'd spend significant time: addictive and melancholic nostalgia. Seeing the dust particles glistening from the sunshine through the window, I looked out finally, and the knowledge that I needed to get going at once was jarringly evident. Microdoses of hope and relief joined forces with despair and stress while I walked back to the sweltering room and awaited my mother's arrival to pick me up, so I could part ways with this war-torn being.

What happens when the wild party ends? Are you to transform like metamorphosis? Will your return to life be as triumphant as you expected it to be, if you even return at all? Or will you be too far gone to prepare a response?

I don't know. I don't know, yet. I just need time to sit back and think before my twisted brain trust realizes where I am. That is, one step ahead, for a change. If I can return to the ground and find a place of refuge, I'll get back to you with honest answers to your many valid questions. Then, all right we will be.

To you, Son,
I'm with you today.
I'll be with you tomorrow.
The downpours, along with the strife.
This glistening, dichotomous fortune
you are now aware of.
Those people I gave to you ... they lost when you lost.
Without feeling and tears, you surely
perished and thirsted.
But I'll fill your cup to overflowing. I'll take care of you.
I'll keep my promises—the ones you see
glimpses of every now and again.
I'll renew your mind and provide clarity of your purpose.
Come. Walk with me on the trail I've blazed.
Just for you.
My vision. A perfect creation.
With real inevitability of greatness awaiting.
—*God*

Mind Relics: Series III

1. "He that getteth wisdom loveth his own soul: he that keepeth understanding shall find good" (Proverbs 19:8).
2. "Wash yourself clean. With simplicity, with humility, with indifference to everything but right and wrong. Care for other human beings. Follow God" (Book 7, #31, *Meditations*).
3. To establish and maintain peace with others, all while being the furthest from ignorant. The mind and soul are to be above hate and above offenses.
4. The art of living boils down to the choices we make. And a blot it would be to allow fear to anchor in, deciding the outcomes of our existences.
5. If not now, then. Mysteries lurking in the shadows along with hidden feelings may soon be revealed to us. Time will tell.
6. Ultimately, we pay the price for the lifestyle we choose to live. Self-strife is inevitable, and one of two primary prices tends to be reflected upon by elders: The strain of regret or the strain of discipline. The choice is ours.
7. Aging too fast or consequently an old soul with a new perspective?
8. We must be real with our people. The truth will have consequences attached, but the variables attached to deceit have a far uglier, unjust underbelly.
9. Wake up feeling like a million bucks today? Wise to invest some of that energy in others who may feel penniless inside. Reciprocate positive energy, and you will not need to be concerned if it's harnessed or not.

10. We are skilled actors with cloaks hiding how we actually feel. Without knowing what others are going through in private, it's essential to treat people with compassion and respect.
11. Why is it so easy for individuals close or far to see us clearly? Because they're exposed to the very details we are not. A self-awareness perspective may be the missing piece to your unsolvable puzzle.

    Clean, sort, and distinguish meaningful scenes in your past tense.

    Transcend your body and delve into your mind.
12. To run from God is to run from yourself. We are the same species. We share the same needs. An inherent struggle to escape the ordered truth of your behavior and God's plan is present always, yet variables in our power are exercised to deflect the truth.
13. All this pressurized weight on our shoulders. Love and hate to admit that it's almost entirely self-inflicted.
14. Trends come and go, but gratitude is here to stay, so deem what you have to be enough. It probably is. Never any requirement to intentionally sabotage yourself by appealing to outside social forces. Striving for self-mastery originating from self-love will satisfy and allow compassion to flow through the floodgates.
15. The soul is for us. The spirit that fills the soul is for us. The heart is for us. The mind, however, can be with us and against us simultaneously. Relentlessly warping what is real and what is only versioned, playing tempting tricks, and tainting our hearts and spirits detrimentally.

16. Which thoughts are real, and which are not? Should worry be placed on this thought or that thought?

    As pressure creates diamonds, intense self-reflection often provides clarity. The clarity to find answers and eventually, peace. With faith, mindfulness, and prayer at the helm, your history will resist repeating itself.
17. Even if your demons respect you, do not be deceived by them. They take your mind and life and shackle it to the things under the sun. Nothing new there. Instead, through persecution, trade them for protecting angels, and in time darkness will fade away.
18. No outsider can save you. The only thing strong enough to penetrate the armor of your mind is itself. Just as the mind has the power to dim even the best life has to offer, it also has wherewithal to prevail over the formidable forces of distress and battles you are fighting now.
19. "Think of yourself as dead. You have lived your life. Now take what's left and live it properly" (Book 7, #56, *Meditations*).
20. And that which we wanted and revered as gain for so long no longer enters our mind. Overvaluing what was never intended for us and not valuing the many blessings provided enough.
21. Our world is landscaped with many dualities, so here's an even split: What if?

    You have nothing to prove to others. You have everything to prove to yourself.
22. Witnessed elders recover in their later years, going on to achieve clarity and peace beautifully, so do not be

discouraged or feel you have "failed" at life while your blood still runs young.

23. Pursue better for yourself and your loved ones without motive to shade others along the way. Winning in private is still winning.
24. Rock bottom appears different for each person. Struggles, trials, and tribulations vary for everybody. Avoid placing too little empathy for others who are plagued by things that do not plague us.
25. Yesterday was yesterday, and we should fashion it to history. But if unfinished business remains in it and is carried onward, our priceless today will soon become yet another missed opportunity—just another blurry twenty-four.
26. No book to be judged by its cover and no person to be preliminarily judged by their appearance on the surface; many of our significant truths are in places of well-guarded, pressurized depth.
27. "And be not conformed to this world: but ye be transformed by the renewing of your mind, that ye may prove what is that good, and acceptable, and perfect, will of God" (Romans 12:2).
28. Time and energy would be wasted if revenge is the mission. Vengeance and injustice are not ours to facilitate.
29. The gloomy morning after and the feelings that coincide with it are seldom explored—mostly the climax and vibe of the main event. Let this be the morning after the party. The harsh awakening to all that is to be regretted and dealt with from compounding issues

and wrongdoing. Missing the mark, but nonetheless, renewal is the centerpiece in our lives' structural blueprints.

30. We cannot be fake and perfect still, but if our connected subject of thought and feeling is genuine, it is much closer to attainable goodness. That's all we can ask for, reasonably.
31. Time after time, stuck is the mental state. But all it may take is one feeling, one testament, one moment, or one human interaction to release you from it. If any and all of the above are true and real, you should not find yourself lost and vice shackled.
32. Despite all sinning that we've done, currently do, and will surely do in the future, we're undeservingly forgiven by God's mercy. It's our time to enlighten and inspire to lessen the time others spend in a hellish mind state here on earth using our given charms.
33. Meaningful progress is not necessarily visible to outsiders. Demeanor alterations are forged from within. It's real trauma behind "cool, calm, and collected" all the same.
34. Standing square and returning a stare bravely at what used to cause you multitudes of mayhem with complete indifference by way of growth—what remarkable and stoic work you've done. For the future, the stories captured in our souls need telling, and the pages in our manuscripts need turning.
35. To see another day is a lovely dream. But where do we go from here? What now? Our next blessed phases will soon be underway, featuring all-new serious

circumstances, but the things in our mind and in our control remain. Only this time with more enhanced lived experience to guide us. Let's paint our remaining phases' pictures vibrantly.

[Therapy—4:15 p.m.]

"Oh, my goodness. That phase probably seems absolutely unreal to you now, I'm sure. If only it was natural for people to gravitate toward the things we bury and fear.

sits back in chair

All said and done, though, I can't really say that I'm at all surprised by the "descent," as you call it. Unfortunately, you've described a fair share of the youthful and developed human experience. There's no softening that right now, either."

"Yeah, for sure. In all reality, that's exactly right. No matter how much you paint the past to feel a certain way for other people, the truth's gonna come out eventually. It always does. Yeah, we all have our ongoing personal issues, but it's crazy. Sometimes I can't help but think that maybe I just lucked out and got somewhere close to the optimal amount of trauma early on. I don't know. One thing I do know is that life is too short to sit around trying to figure everything out by ourselves. Doing that, you'd pass on before you even got the chance to contribute and live."

"Certainly. And finding ways to ensure that stress is controllable for young people is proving more difficult by the decade. On that topic, meaningful mental health awareness programs across the nation are in practice now, but the most readily available mechanism for improvement is simply to interact with companions. Family, friends, coworkers—practically everybody can serve as a therapeutic figure in some sort of way."

leans forward while hand-gesturing assertively

"What's been said earlier doesn't need readdressing, but I will say that making your afflictions and sins "real" with no intoxication or oblivion involved, even if it's just jotting them down and figuring out how to deal with them instead of always compensating, coping, and loathing based on behavior makes a world of difference. This being maybe nothing more than an example of that is reason enough to exist, in my opinion. Uh, so long as chaos stirs our worlds individually, we may need or desire something to cling to for a specific perspective on something, and if this is that, then awesome. Definitely not the be-all and end-all, but hey, it's what can be offered at this moment. I'm so grateful that everything turned out this way and that the people won. No souls were sold during this process, and nobody was expensed because of the reluctant exploration of mine, and so many others,' neuro vices."

"That's wonderful to hear, Milo. What an incredibly effective session this has been. We're looking forward to officially hearing what led to your advancements in thought processes and where our deep conversations may take people outside of this room today. On behalf of my colleagues here at the office, I also want to thank you for carrying out your vision for this healing project. The fourth phase already promises a completely different vibe, and quite honestly, it makes me question if I'm ready to hear it and what phase number I'm in right now, too."

smiles and gazes out the window

"You know, this entire experience has been so real, so enlightening, and so cathartic. It's honestly a testament to how no one goes it alone out here. We need each other.

Like, what's a perfectly manifested vision if the people God placed in your life aren't there to see it come true alongside you?

exhales

Yeah.

It's time to remember again."

lowers heart rate

eases mind

reveals heart and soul

PHASE IV

MENTAL RENAISSANCE

Demons for Angels

All right we will be, indeed. How we've only dreamed of this cerebral-squalor-to-splendor moment so long and to now have it come to fruition—no outsider can tell us this victorious feeling is not well deserved, so let it sink in. We've got the blues on the run, and we've definitively crossed into a disparate mental territory. Paradise. Or rather, the closest thing to paradise available to our earthly minds. A euphoric space wherein the mind is nourished, not overcome with nonactualized constructs of our efforts being meaningless. In this distinctly zen domain, we are courageous enough to view ourselves and our surroundings in a new light and as they truly are, as opposed to bending them with our free will, which may not be so free, as we've learned the hard way. Imagining a domain where those in it do not naturally return to their respective views following consideration is pointless now. This is that space. Material goods we once revered are dim in relation to this vivid mind realm that so graciously supplies plentiful "no longers" and permits past tenses to strike and flow through our yesterdays as if there was no tomorrow. To describe a magical, yet very real marketplace for ideas and philosophies to be shared with one another for too long would be a mistake, but an understanding that finding truth and annihilating bad habits are not feared in and around these parts must be common knowledge to extract all that is marketed here. As you are able, please leave behind all worry, pain, and hatred here before we explore any more of this wondrous age. You will not be needing any more of it, anyway.

Interchangeable are life and mystery for humankind, and thus, we navigate through our years ignorantly thinking we possess intelligence regarding what's around most corners and exactly how we will respond to whatever it may be. Besides that idea, we gravitate toward an abyss of unease and hopelessness, for what is around corners is far beyond the breadth of our insight and control. Additionally, our choices entering the mix make the mystery more interesting. Within the abundant cluster of challenging choices, or life, are cinematic chronological phases composing your physical existence. If what I wrote a few sentences back is true, and life and mystery go hand in hand, it would be fair to declare that you may be headed unequivocally toward a period of your life you would have never pictured or thought was possible. Unimaginable. For better or worse, transitions seamlessly connect eras having absolutely no business being adjacent to one another, like my third and this fourth. We've no choice but to take some losses with phases and accept the photogenic smiles and unsightly frowns in all sectors of our distinct journeys. If what I wrote a few sentences back is true, and life and mystery go hand in hand simultaneously, it would be fair to declare that you may be headed unequivocally toward a period of your life you not only embrace altruistically but see clearer than you've ever pictured or thought was possible. Unimaginable. For better or worse, enough subtle wisdom infiltrates our minds, and often we tie loose ends, abandon long-held raging grudges, and perceive nature as a whole new network of God-created wonder and beauty. Before demonstrating an example of life and mystery further, cheers all around are ordained in this fourth phase. We made it here triumphantly and triumph through transition is on full display in this lush mind realm. Let's open our possibilities to change and entertain comfort arising from a neurotic trance, even if being shaken awake is the entry mechanism to your age of mental and spiritual enlightenment. As always, do not forget to stop and take a look around, but something tells me we'll be here for quite a while.

As melodies complement life's flow and overall aura from different platforms, a euphonious reference may be ideal to figuratively represent this phase change. Because music sounds better at these precise mental coordinates, most of the time when I excitedly discuss an album with somebody close or far, I think, *Ah, I wish I could hear that song for the first time again!* The truth is that the most memorable moments are those we simply cannot expect. Not knowing what lurks around every corner is a marvelous element of life, in general. There are special and appropriate spaces for both, but which would you personally prefer—to anticipate and experience an otherworldly transition between two songs you already know and love, or be pleasantly blindsided by a flowing record transition that you're hearing for the first time, with no preconceived notion or expectation? Reminiscing, I was at a highly awaited stadium concert with a group of friends, and midway through the symphony-like show, mystical tones filled the air we breathed, drum and synthesizer patterns were smoothly altered, angelic samples entered our eardrums, dopamine released in our bloodstreams from raw euphoria, and circular-oriented light beams pierced through the inky, clear skies. Almost completely entranced by the ambiance and storytelling of the display amid the other fifty-five thousand or so folks sharing the identical wave energy, I came to find that light beams were beginning to shine through to my future, mentally. From this point onward, through the reveal of our souls, it's possible to view, or rather listen, to past, present, and future life as if it's a cohesive album with tones matching our all-encompassing vibes. A sound-scaped dream. Within the orchestration was breaking free from hard-mounted impairments that consisted of many a bewildering situation, especially the neurosis extended to whether airplanes would crash due to the light show glowing from the ground to what seemed like an atmospheric portal from a uniting human experience. So, this is the space we find ourselves in, I suppose. Tugged in two or more opposing directions and caught in a world where worlds collide. We must make up our minds and select a side to allow the flourishing creation of revolutionary things following testing tribulation.

As your renaissance tour ambassador, I again welcome you to the conclusion of this particular odyssey, which is only the beginning of a brighter, more vivid era for us, together. The dark ages have surely passed. As trades, realizations, and manifestations blend in a relatively short time, our minds are in a specialized capacity for renewal, or rebirth, if you will. Yes. All the good glory is laid out on the table for us. The claiming of it is completely dependent on your choices right here and right now.

If you've been wondering where the borderline is located, here it is. Giving more and taking less instead of strictly picking and choosing because the school year was complete, I still became disgruntled and overwhelmed after seeing the sheer number of belongings in need of unpacking upon the jovial return drive from the dormitory. Lugging my typical, ridiculous behavioral tendencies along with the three large containers once storing a huge amount of cereal, frustration led me to believe that a repeat of the previous year's panicky summer was inbound, even after a couple of adequate semesters. After listening to my mother's calming logic, I slept soundly, but not before brutal reconciliation with myself over the foolish pursuit of unreasonable appearance "perfection" in various facets of mundane daily life. A cut-and-dry choice between two-paced lifestyles was inevitable. I was finished stalling on that front. While working and trying my best to balance important business, above anything, I wanted calmness and ease after much chaos and difficulty in self-growth. With a plan to make it a point to attend Sunday service and delve into biblical readings more consistently, slowly the dry spell of reassured blessings was replenished. Living with considerable distance between Jesus and what I knew He envisioned for me played an integral role in self-hatred because there was a potent sense that I was partaking in a mindset that was not in congruence with the truth and my truths, personally. As weeks passed, it became clear that proactively seeking assurance and faith by God's grace found in the Bible was going to deliver me out of a neuro-vice-positioned rut of life, as opposed to creating false truths and attempting to justify them as an unrighteous young adult.

Can one really be free being caught in cahoots with pleasure and wild thoughts while choosing to represent a stoic and compassion-honed lifestyle in 2023 and beyond? Probably not. To recognize there may or may not be an absurdly fine line between flexing liberties given to us and downright living wrong. Workday after workday, I would lounge on our front porch to stare into nature and consider everything that arose in my now idled-down brain following years of being strongly advised to slow down, take time off, and live more loosely. Privately following those instructions, I held breaths that I did not know my lungs were capable of while listening to music and sipping passionfruit herbal tea like a traditional old soul and arrived at my honest, natural persona. By the second, I gained new perspectives by psychoanalyzing the lyrics to a song from one of my favorite albums and was in shock that I could relate so directly to a testament that involved seeking a way out of one's head no matter the cost. I prayed for a lasting answer and for other people my age who are treading similar water with mental illness struggles. The final melancholic, yet soothing moments of the introduction track played, and after disconnecting my headphones, I enjoyed hearing birds chirp and returned to form playing the lone yard games I used to pass time with before social media adjusted focus and intentions. It's refreshing to spend time alone and reset given life's stress. Just getting back to basics. We require that, and as for me, that's all I did, because I was genuinely satisfied and not fully enveloped by income and image exclusively. How many calls and texts have I declined and excused from friends who invited me to spend time with them for a while because they missed me? I don't know, but enough. I felt guilt from telling them no and that I would not be there, but considering the real healthy strides I was making and that that my vibe and valued interests were no longer in near alignment with theirs, it was as if I had no choice but to politely remove myself, because my growth was apart from most others I associated with. It's only natural. To be blunt, I only wanted to be alone with God in prayer and with like-minded individuals at church, or with family members who were alongside me through all these phases. A future with aggregate schemes and plots was of no interest to me anymore. I suddenly deemed them unworthy of significant attention.

To be free: to not be pulled in two or more opposing directions and not be positioned too comfortably in a place of temporary pleasure, lust, and consequently, regret. And to think differently, not for the sake of trying hard to be different, but to pursue good for yourself and your people. If that's too much to ask for as decent ones just trying to move forward to justice, we would be unfairly treated, right? Well, with the rage buried inside seemingly fading away bit by bit, I found that the compounding mistakes I'd made had been undeservingly forgiven when I reached out and emptied my mind and heart to the Lord first. The shoulder load lightened significantly because of it. I took a near 180-degree dispositional turn over a summer, but various sources of social influence may not have minded to see me and many other young aspiring people remain in the fast lane to a long life of private self-hatred and despair. Never mind them. We cannot dictate their behavior, as it's leveraged by taught, potent corruption. In other news, by way of many empowering chats and sermons with families and pastors at Bible church, it was evident that genuine people have your back if and when you need it, and I grasped that nearly every major object my mind obsessed over for half a decade was problematic in ways more detrimental than originally illustrated mentally, as psychological plagues trickled their way to reach far beyond sociological complications. The result of those trickles: an ornately ordered mess. A life of only vanity, pleasure, and overly abundant riches at the expense of others is no utopia at all. That reads more like a campaign of disguised sorrow. Concluding that you were flawed and weak in thought when it mattered hits hard. Even more difficult to accept, those individuals you used to be so close with—you will most likely have to move on from them. Philosophies, attitudes, and perceptions of the world are wildly contrasting now, and there's a high probability of that placement remaining, the way it must be at certain times. That's a primary facet of maturation. Telling you what it is by telling you what it is not once again. To be free: to not give in to worldly temptation and obsess over ransoming compulsions and not be afraid to politely decline misaligned engagements during times of healing. To be free: to transcend mental strain and complete execution of the 180-degree turnaround of renewal and ultimately decide to trade your demons for angels.

In a world such as the one we inhabit, it can be all too easy to find yourself lost in an eclectic web of desires. And all too easily comes the directional changing of our minds once we've obtained the tangible good and accolades we pursued forever, seemingly. Satisfaction prefers to come wrapped with a bow and ribbon, but there always seems to be a catch. The journey would be all too easy if it wasn't littered with guilt, self-doubt, embarrassment, and lack of credibility when arguments beg a bolster. We desire minds at peace, not at war. But what if all you were familiar with was melancholic war and nostalgic blues? A sort of survivor's guilt may present itself. You may find you were addicted to being sorrowful, and once you no longer carry that emotion in excess, you'll experience not only growing pains, but a faulty esteem system. Esteem is often drained outright by a normally closed valve, not filtered, so you understand and accept that most of your wounds after the adolescent responsibility cut-off point were self-caused. And your wounds—yes, yours—they undeniably prove that your demons are nothing to be messed with. Yet, they tempt and try everything in their power to pull you back in an opposing, detrimental direction, or what was once your default state. This, dear friends, is nothing more than an expected obstruction in the healing process. Simply because you desire to design and live with a cleaner disposition and you're near it does not in any sense mean that your trials in life are drawing to a close. So, remain as strong as you've ever been. Hark back to why you decided to resist your default state in the first place. Pray tranquilly but battle evil spirits as if your future depends on it, and when that time presents itself, you'll know. Trust it. Do not be afraid to march to the beat of your own drum if you must. If it's a decisive laceration you must make between revelry and serenity, remember that the place you least wish to remember is the place you may need to pay a visit to evade tricks up the sleeves of those who envy you from afar, accompanying your trauma.

When I was between the ages seven and thirteen, my father enjoyed listening to an anecdotal-based radio show called *Unshackled* whenever we drove through town. Undoubtedly, due to repeated scenes during youth, that word stuck with me through adolescence. Not once did I stop and dissect the variables surrounding a shackle of any kind, or even what the word personified, though. Having matured, I now empathize with the most real of stories once stagnant in the back of my head courtesy of tough times' facilitation. And that I hope for you, as well. Moreover, because I was transferring universities, I hoped to break away from my apparent mind shackles and make the unconventional transition to a life young people do not typically embrace from one that is. Reaching the point of no return regarding caring deeply about how others perceive me, I both priced and valued peace fairly and decided to do everything in my power to remove and discard the disguise, abandon the developed facade, and focus on kindling a genuine enthusiasm for living. For good. Appearing the same on the outside, unfazed and serious, the inside became a different story: faithful and content instead of spiteful and ruffled. Past immoral tricks at my disposal required disposal, as well. Once enlightened on the mental construct of ego and accepting that it is capable of more than familial destruction, meditating and humbling myself enough to admit that the character created in my mind does not exist in any form proved perilous, as I was so comfortable with observing life utilizing ego as the lens to operate regularly when alone or with people.

Time has an interesting way of ticking when you seriously consider yourself trending onward and upward. Before you know it, the period of initial motivational overdrive is over and a concerning void is all but irrelevant. Let's face it, fatigue sets in. Look at what we're tackling head-on. We should cut ourselves some slack. At this rate, merely maintaining peace and order mentally is challenging enough. Life is not getting any less complex for anybody. Or so it seems. With each of us hauling around differing quantities of indebtedness, weighty emotional baggage, grief, and the knowledge of blown opportunities, the faith we have in the guiding angels we traded for must be structurally sound to right our wrongs and distinguish between rubbish and priceless missing puzzle pieces to reflect for as long as we live.

Reparations

> "And to everybody listening, what I have for you
> is nothing to be misconstrued or diluted! It's not
> your typical, light reading material for recreational
> use while relieving yourselves! It meditates on life,
> psychological warfare, spiritual warfare, and many
> other forces under the sun to be reckoned with!
> Have a dance to these soundscapes if you like!"
>
> —A nearby Renaissance promoter

Ha ha. All right. Anyway, as I was saying, the people here welcome deep thought, but I cannot say the same for all outsiders. Well, if they've come to pass in this kind of phase, there's no concern, but if they have yet to feel the need to improve themselves on an ambitious path more rightly, then time will dictate their justice on its own. Speaking of justice: emotional justice, or emotional reparations, are in the works as act two of this new world's order. Adequate trading has taken place. It's time for a prolific realizing age to remedially sanctify what once was a mind in desperate need of reform. Is there any treasure in lieu of the time we wasted away? Perhaps indirectly, or unrelated, but if emotional justice is obtained responsibly in good health, what does it matter if the mind is to be over it?

You see, now that we've resided here for ample reflection to occur, assessing foundational status is on our dockets. Cerebrums are out of order with the inability to receive replacement cells for years and hippocampi are utterly wiped out. I mean, let's be real—our memory stood no chance, to begin with, given the outlook of daily life. To wrap up, amygdalae are seized and still have billowing flames, even considering how much time has passed since our emotional warfare origins. So, as we waltz through this dreary compartment of an otherwise breathtaking landscape, let's despise the ugliness of our individual situations and appreciate the raw power it took to produce such broken mental states. These networks need redesigning and expansion. These impulses need controlling. These emotions need programming, and these habitual nuances need rework. Needless to say, we've got our work cut out for us.

Instead of lying on our backsides wondering where it all went wrong and victimizing ourselves over circumstances in which we knew better, on behalf of those who wish for your growth, I invite each one of you to walk with accountability. To take steps in the general direction of correcting wrongs and claiming responsibility. This is arguably—no, wait, this *is* the most difficult period for any of us to linger in. Reverting to our old ways of loss in thought is tempting. However, we are on the other side now. Going back would only taint our minds, hearts, and souls. We've been shown spirits of the Renaissance, albeit a touch too advanced for us to fully understand currently, but either way, the resources we need to improve are at our fingertips, literally.

To segue, since I was adapting to a vastly different urban playground and university, attempting to reduce stress levels and make the most out of the all-new experience took slight priority over mental health progress. Not for too long, though, because action gave me plenty of time alone and thus plenty of time to psychoanalyze behavior and image from a third-person perspective. As the season changed in favor of purple knuckles and slick grounds, I began attending a similar Bible church near the university. Although social anxiety was still hanging on by a thread, the teachings directly from God's word penetrated my humble and broken exterior and entered my heart, mind, and soul. Each Sunday, another few verses hit me and challenged the topics I thought I had covered soundly. Accompanying each message was a wise and fresh testament calming me while encouraging me to think about life alternatively. To be open to the possibility of true wealth, including a person's burden, by renewing the mind forthrightly and allowing subsequent trust to rest on the shoulders of Jesus's unique plan for our lives upon salvation. To sit down and realize that you and I are children of God first. Ever learning, ever growing, and ever blessed to have been taken care of decently. It's simply what has to be done to gain assurance of lasting peace. All this time was spent endeavoring on separate business ventures, but I was too prideful to admit that His plan was, is, and will be more glorious.

As for you all, I do not know whether brokenness or pride was the roadblock. That is for you to discover. What we can do is support our people and pray for each of their renewals. The fate of the universe is not in our hands, and just the heftiness of our own dealings is enough to trouble us, as we know. So, lift them up in prayer. Place them on an almighty power other than are soon to be repaired cerebrums. Our plots and schemes may benefit us in the short run, but what and who is ordered in our lives is at the mercy of something much more massive and it's appropriate to be feared.

They preach to you. They preach to you, and you hear that all it takes is patience. Once heavily involved in the healing development process, I would not necessarily disagree. That crystal-clear sight comes through and by patience, all the instances in which angels protected you come to attention. It took all but a few hours to realize how lucky I am to have had guys and gals placed into my story amid all the fugazi and numbing trials. If it were not for their company, humor, and uplifts, all the bleaker this anecdote may have been. But we do not need to plague ourselves with those experiences any more than for reflective purposes. It's over. We've won. We've come and we've conquered. All that's left to be done is everything we could not complete or think of completing prior to our lucrative trade of demons for angels.

We progress, we face adversity both bravely and weakly, and we transcend our minds—the same minds sworn to provide beneficial results for us but are destined to lead us to transgression. Perhaps on the same level, we witness firsthand surroundings, or this mind realm, in complete newness. We exhibit changes in our attitudes regarding thanksgiving, meditation, and the value of clarity and peace. We actively seek out opportunities in disguise, and let the truth fend for itself like the lion that it is. We desire and make efforts to repay timely debts to society with letters on a page, words on a screen, phrases in a speech, and stories in the memories of other people who've struggled with similar types of ingrained damage and neurological vices their entire lives. We define words to illustrate the impact correctly defined expressions have on a meaningful life's eulogy. We know a eulogy is not necessary for us, yet. Our reparations are never complete. It's an ongoing process. However, the sooner we arrive at an up-and-running mental status, the sooner we can arrive in others' lives and influence as nature intended. We can see.

Following another successful semester, thankfully, this vision was officially conceived. Platters with burgers and fries were cleared along with my mind. My family members noticed this given the collisions of hundreds of psychological grippings occurring simultaneously. We struck clarity of a certain spirited purpose for our special moment here. Inspiration is truly a thing of beauty, but the knowledge that the existence of this matter for others being reasonable catapulted the vision to a level potent enough to make me question the task in front of me. We are never tasked with spiritual missions we cannot successfully carry out, though. In fact, I never prayed so deeply for direction and usage of strength after the epiphany. The initial weeks of project development were taxing, to say the least, as nightly nightmares and terrifying awakenings blasted positive thoughts to try and relinquish any chance of fulfilling this vision mentally. I came to find out that those daunting nightmares were the attempts by my army of remaining disgruntled demons once accustomed to wreaking havoc in my amygdala. Those types of resistant barriers will arise to keep us blocked and terminate our journey to joyfulness, but we must push through. Call their bluff and trust in the path laid out for us. We can see and fulfill.

Such incredible sight was instilled and still, there are scenes in every phase we do not see coming, including this next kind. Throughout the mental and emotional reconstructive ride, traditional physical work remained steady, especially during the hectic holiday season. Working in the same position as earlier in a different store, my task was to assist two young gentlemen, Oliver and Leo, with unloading and organizing a sizable frozen truckload. As I neared their location, I wondered if there would be any awkwardness looming because we had not worked with each other directly. Fortunately for the three of us, awkwardness was not an appropriate feeling to describe our interaction. Upon completion of a comedian-like bit, conversationally, we transitioned to a deeper, more genuinely connected zone of the interaction. We shared and discovered private details with one another quickly, and Oliver told me that he and Leo were also in the process of self-improvement, only theirs was in the form of rehabilitation from drug and alcohol addiction-related struggles. Although I cannot relate to their trials, we all were passionately surfing the same wave and bounced wisdom and reminiscent moments of triumph and tragedy off each other. In addition to the beginning of more meaningful friendships, Oliver, Leo, and I acted as assets for each other in our respective pursuits of mental health. This spontaneous, recovery-oriented exchange of refreshing and valuable thought between Oliver and me emerged as a newfound pillar in each of our mind-reparation projects.

A Conversation with Oliver

Milo: "And over time, um, I just realized that to get peace you have to go out of your comfort zone and really work for it. Before, it was all about finding the wrong things to cling to and taking the easy way out of my head. Now, I've kinda accepted that triumph and comfort are not connected. It will only be there if your work is at the level it needs to be at, both mentally and spiritually."

Oliver: "Right. Part of what I'm doing right now is going through "the big book" and organizing, like, the part I played in the destruction of myself and other relationships, reaching out to apologize and take responsibility and fix a lot of things that got lost these last few years. Actually, next week, I'm speaking on a panel at a conference I was invited to about my experiences at my lowest to here seven months sober. It's gonna be hard to describe what life is like now, but I'll find a way to relate it to people."

Milo: "That's awesome, man. Sounds like it'll be a massive opportunity. And yeah, presenting a vision is ridiculous sometimes. Few will truly understand or see it unless you carry it out. So, what's been the most difficult part of your recovery in the past seven months? Was it looking to God or trying to rewire your mind to resist relapsing?"

Oliver: "Uh, definitely resisting the urge to go back to my lifestyle for the first couple months, and then once I was somewhat clear of that, understanding and accepting that, like, "Oh, this is what it's like to be sober again. Not everybody needs to drink when drinks are around and available" type of thing. Ha ha. What about you?"

Milo: "Facts. Like you say, resisting the urge to allow my compulsions to control my behavior and feeling split between a normal life and complete chaos was the hardest to deal with. I knew the contrasts in everything well, like, lofty goal success doesn't normally go together with getting distraught about dog hair on clothes and furniture, you know. Anyway, through writing and planning, I've been able to note that because there was so much pent-up aggression and unfinished business from however many years is the reason behind why my exterior was pristine and in perfect order. Neurotic on the inside and stoic on the outside. It was all a facade. All a compensation."

Oliver: "Yeah, for sure, man. I get that. What I try to tell my housemates is how much of a painstaking process all this actually is and that even if you weren't as messed up as I was, you still could be getting more out of yourself for people around you. Life doesn't have to be awful. We can choose to make it better. You just have to be stronger than you ever thought possible and get out of body to look at things from a different perspective."

Milo: "Hmm, I've never heard it explained like that ever, but it's true, man. To give you some perspective, too, I was having conversations about life being a game hopelessly and how I was avoiding relationships because of my issues, and you know, here we are a year later, having this one because of real stories. If that isn't the power of the Holy Spirit, then I honestly don't know what is. Turning it around took a lot of effort, but of course, it's worth every impossible minute."

Oliver: "The grind continues, homie. Stay with it. I've never heard anybody say they regret working hard at improving their lives, especially for the sake of people close. Need to focus on building people up, not tearing 'em down."

Milo: "Yeah, and we'll be ready for all that we have to claim once we're done around here. Until then, take it easy. Burritos on Friday, right?"

Oliver: "Yeah. You got it. Peace out, brotha."

Moments in time pass so quickly that it's best not to blink. We try to cherish what we can while we can. Elegant keys, reverbed flutes, and gorgeous accompanying string instrumentals flowed through my increasingly established, zen mind while awaiting sundown by the nearby river. Gazing at the water's reflection with sunglasses awning the blinding glare, I slowly removed and pocketed them. Seeing the mirror image, I accepted the raw truth in my eyes and that this is where self-love took me. No longer on a borderline. No longer numb. Considering the scene, it's fair to imagine confusion arising in the minds of passersby near the piers, like, *What in the world is going on in this guy's head?* Since much of life and the people living it are a mystery and will remain that way, I returned calmly to seated daydreaming and decided to give both my parents a call to update them on the status of my reflective writing and describe intricate details comprising the vision I'd been attempting to make a reality for others. Rehabilitating and breaking down defective walls in our diseased and disturbed minds require and further kindle brutal honesty with ourselves. People will take notice of the results originating from that honesty. They, too, can find and experience revelation in reparation.

Ahead of everything coming full circle here
in crunch time, this is my final question to
you in this reconstructive territory:

*If this mind realm's lead shepherd handed you one
hundred pages to draft whatever you wished for the
utilization of society at large, what would you put forth?*

As we discreetly wonder when time will run out in our current phases and current lives, let's remember how our Renaissances took shape. Mine had become closer to goodness upon the pursuit of assurance and truth back at the hotel while seeking to uplift another person from the book that provided me the greatest amount of peace. I wish the same for you and all those you'll inspire once they've been enlightened by your purpose and having achieved a high form of cerebral freeness. How it feels like a bittersweet wake for your past self. The transitional era has worked its nearly inconceivable magic as promised, and you can expect some missing puzzle pieces to meditate with before we venture into our upcoming phases individually.

Thank you all for demonstrating that visions, dreams, and even nightmares can become reality if you're willing to collect and embrace the many puzzle pieces off the floor and seal them in position as mind relics. You have to unlock your past voluntarily in order to lock up a future intended for you and only you—one that you do not even know exists. When the hour arises and you are called on to speak on behalf of something immensely real, you'll know. You'll know simply because you possess a special channel, a pure spirit filling a soul previously neglected and invisible to yourself and others. The mind is right. The mind is renewed. We just needed to examine it wholeheartedly and think beyond only our beings. Now each of our destinies wants us back on track.

Missing Peaces

To those of you genuinely trying your hardest to make a way in this complex world and who seem to constantly run into mental roadblocks, there are a handful of think pieces I will share if you'd like. Simply put, there's just so much uncertainty. Endeavoring into the unknown as mortals with, but mostly without, crucial compartmentalization of variables our lives possess for us forging ahead. Deep thoughts tend to produce deeper blues, but maybe that's only because they've not been solidified as true mind relics, yet. Regardless of the position we are in during our unpromised collection of years, we will inevitably cascade into the following sequences if and when we actively try to explore the possibility of an improved life for ourselves and influential souls around us. It's a trip. Absolutely. Remember that when we get to where we're going, we rarely think about the significance of the outcome, but we do think about the people we sojourn alongside and the vivid experiences we shared. We now know the flagship outlet to access those is self-reflection. Come to find out, there are pieces and processes to our peace puzzles demanded by our minds to proceed boldly beyond this Renaissance.

I present to you various missing peaces: ten distinct reflective testaments intended for real-life application. It's been a pleasure serving as your ambassador. Until next time.

Visions

Although it may seem as though you've stumbled upon an absolute curse with the conception of your bespoke vision for the future, notice how it's classified as a vision and not a far-fetched delusion or forgettable dream. You're not a crazy person for having a unique idea. Do not let outsiders dissuade you from following your sight or persuade you into thinking your plan will never work. Tunnel vision, or getting into a certain zone, is very real. If you've been located and chosen to organize a particular venture and have to decide whether or not to sacrifice some things, or maybe all things in pursuit of it, consider yourself fortunate. Many individuals would give everything for an opportunity like yours, so the pressure on your shoulders, self-inflicted or not, is to be welcomed and harnessed while striving to fulfill what few people, if any, see so clearly.

Disconnecting from the ultimate completion of any given concept is often required to freely entertain every consideration and not fall in love with a "boxed-in" plan set before reality trickles in. Settle comfortably into humility and brokenness in and from your mind and heart. Accept that hate is not a facilitator of any kind of visionary success. While working toward a goal intelligently and diligently, you must make a conscious distinction in philosophy. Will you believe that you were located for a reason and that you would not have been chosen if you were incapable of finding a way through all the tests in development? Or will you back down because self-doubt drowned faith and trust in yourself and specific prospects? Of course, because your care is genuine, self-doubt perils will assert themselves, but that is the exact point at which goal discipline assumes control. Just as discipline assumes control when motivation is lacking, your spirit can assume control when you're willing to give your time and one-of-a-kind charms for good. For God's vision. Respect and allow mental and spiritual discipline power to carry that vision to new heights when drive or desire is insufficient.

Finally, besides thinking grandly, to excel for any significant period of time chasing a naturally occurring complex thought, derealization must be disintegrated and nonexistent in your innovative mind field. It's fairly obvious, but if there is even a flicker of nihilism or consideration that the past, present, and future human existence does not matter or is merely a basis for easily replaceable pleasure day after day, you and the vision are destined to be flooded with discouragement without lasting hope. Protect your energy! All it takes is the optimal blend of optimistic and pessimistic attitudes to form a healthy undertaking. The most minuscule of alterations in your mindset, goal setting, and communication could very well have existential effects pertaining to the fulfillment of your ambitions. Allow God to direct you in times of struggle, because there will definitely be times of struggle. No matter the scope or prevalence of your vision(s), be open to seeking assistance from others, as well. Those individuals may offer the perspective you were in desperate need of to escape a void, if any are present. We're here for one another and we're here to witness and enjoy one another's creations. Passionately abiding by a tailored approach strictly designed for incremental progress, along with following the commitment principles outlined, should reveal a new reality to outsiders who were once a mere bewildering vision.

DND

Profound revelations either cause a desire for complete solitude or to go out and profess all that's been discovered. Both are understandable and necessary, but what occurs in the systematic hours of lonesomeness will determine your outlook on life and if your visions ever come into it. This is the part when you set your devices and align your mentality to "Do Not Disturb," but also designate resources for use during self-reflection and hard work, although those are synonymous. We're humans. Everything negative in our lives is not even close to our fault. Moreover, we need to be willing to think for ourselves without outside attention for adequate time to organize and recuperate our mangled minds.

Mental stimulation and clarity are sparked when you walk alone on a road meant for you. If undisturbed solitude is where you strike the most effective observation, lock yourself into a room and duel with your demons by piecing together and releasing burdensome, chronological causes and effects, if you must. Your ideal mental destination will provide clues to the answer of an appropriate reflection setting. This world offers a slew of flashing distractions to draw you in all at once, but little to no advancements will be made there, specifically. To recover and focus on what needs to be fixed internally. Voluntarily distancing yourself from others for an extended time is often a robust plan when healing is the objective. Friends, family members, and strangers may not grasp what it is that you're trying to reckon for yourself, and that's OK. They have the right to think for themselves as you do, and you cannot control what they perceive you to be by overanalyzing real and hypothetical interactions in the dark all alone.

Focusing and spotting solutions to your personal development issues is only fair, so you should not disregard the idea of a hiatus. Only you can attest to every relevant variable, like what happened in the past, how it affected you, and why things have to be this way now. Do whatever appropriate thing it is you have to conduct reflectionally and extract yourself from the mental woes of yesterday, solo or not. Just ensure disturbances are kept to a minimum as their causes are within your mental jurisdiction. When you set out on your adventure, you recognized things would become arduous and gruesome, sooner or later. Keep composed, find a place to let your guard down, and recharge. Believe it or not, your grandest legacy is still obtainable.

Growing Pains

What's occurring behind the scenes is serious business, and you are beginning to become a force to be reckoned with. Keep that fact firmly in your mind and value your worth. The amount of strength you have inside yet to be unleashed is absurd. But what is a temporary price to be paid after you decide not to sell your soul? One of them is a sparkling gemstone in disguise: hurt stemming from detailed mental and emotional trauma excavation swirled with maturation. Apart from that, growing pains begin to confuse and decelerate your advancements in visionary and reflective negotiations. You'll be punched powerfully with intelligence that who you are becoming is somebody you revere more than the past, but those in and around your circle may not agree and align conceptually with your future endeavors. Letting go is a whole other story in the growing pain chapter. So, in addition to finding out the hard way that you're different now and will be different forever, you may also find that others switch in retaliation, simply because you have transformed despite all real complications. Inconveniently, some others' demons will be flustered by your spirited efforts, which contributes to the list of expectable growing pains.

We are all destined to change and grow in time. If there are individuals who were your closest confidants prior to your self-improvement desire that cannot find it in themselves to support you in the process, they might need to be left behind, respectfully. We're not immune to doubt, hate, gossip, and envy, so you must take a trust-filled stand to distinguish between those who are meant to be present with you continuously and those who cannot offer support in regard to personal breakthroughs. Their time in your episodical life may have run out, and although it's strange and uncomfortable, please understand that growth is produced by fusing voluntary discomfort with honest, courageous considerations like prayer, meditation, and thought.

Challenging your mind's boundaries is like gaining muscle mass. The more time and energy you expend toward figuring out wrongs and relentlessly addressing evil behavior, the more noticeably unbreakable you become. Nothing truly worthwhile is easily obtainable. If it were, everybody would have all their individual plagues repaired sufficiently, and it would always be evident from the outside. Consider mental, emotional, and spiritual exhaustion and soreness a prime indicator of expansion in the right areas and as great steps in the right direction. You'll want nothing more than to tap out and escape the ring of voluntary distress but keep battling. You're doing an adequate job fighting your demons instead of the idea of change. And it is not only at night you take notice of opposites outside. As a matter of fact, you're getting closer.

Duality

To be completely blind to the contrasting tendencies on this earth we call home would prove that a significant piece of this process puzzle is missing. At the end of the day, everybody has thousands of choices to make privately and must be able to coexist with those choices until we pass on. Good and evil, Heaven and hell, or utopia and dystopia, highs and lows, progress and switching, sober and psychedelic, and health and toxicity are misconstrued points of the sharp duality we grasp, but we rarely meditate upon them except in intense dialogue.

Without a shadow of a doubt, by now, you've run

into many a contrast. You must make divisions correctly to resume this journey. Current times can trick you into believing something is gold when really, it's merely fool's gold, or thinking that someone is like a sheep when really that someone is a wolf in sheep's clothing. Your advancements are dependent on honest distinctions between every dual topic to better solidify what you're about and what is worth your undivided attention, energy, and passion. Sifting through the real and fake just might be the most pressing. Not everybody wishes for what is in your best interest, and there's always going to be a flip side to strong arguments, all the same. So, keep watch and anticipate grime on the road to cleanliness.

Your gut feeling is instilled for a sound reason—to guide reasoning efforts in social situations. The decision to abide by it is laid out every time, but I wonder about its success rate and if you listen to it enough. As the line between opposing concepts and directions becomes thinner and thinner, your natural instincts may need to work overtime to direct yourself through complex situations. A blank canvas is a wonderful opportunity, and its idea is quite intriguing. Limitless interactional possibilities with the outside world are all but irrational in this technological age, and you can control exactly how you interact with your canvas, which leads to the question: how will you paint the remainder of your picture?

Rhythm & Tempo

While initially learning to play the game of golf, my father preached the importance of both rhythm and tempo in executing a smooth, controlled swing with every club. As I matured and pondered the variables surrounding my existence more, those applicable and imperative golf swing properties were in my consciousness, and I would constantly remind myself that I ought to operate fluidly, without sudden jerks, in handling daily life's occurrences. What was so beneficial to realize was that as the mind controls the body, the mind also sets the tone of flow transmission to the body. If an optimal pace is not intentionally programmed in your mind, your body will follow any living speed available based on measly observations, and sufficient control over how you function will be lost. Compromised.

To let things unfold naturally, avoid forcing things into existence. Put plainly, life's flow differs for every person. A fast, gripping life that works for one individual may lead to absolute destruction for another. What you must do is set your own pace. Dance to your own favorite records and politely decline the invitation to disrupt your rhythm and tempo. If you successfully operate sternly and swiftly, let it be. If you successfully operate methodically and leisurely, let that be. Embrace your flow and acknowledge the diversity and subjectivity in our respective adventures.

Fleeting time places many uncontrollable aspects directly in front of us, but if one thing is for sure, it's that you have full say in the speed at which you live. You can choose to increase or decrease your pace in certain lanes to suit certain situations. Also, feel free to select a useful momentum you think would best fit your current phase and even go back to your arsenal of flows to claim more desirable results with future shots you take in life. It's so frustrating when a disconnect arises between life's demands and our capabilities, and if you do not know where those capabilities rest, you cannot possibly expect to somehow select the best flow. How neat it is to find parallels and apply musical terms to golf and then to living. How interesting it is to articulate the togetherness of many seemingly unrelated things. Perhaps we're more connected in vision pursuit than we thought!

Butterfly Effect

What if we resided in a universe where every decision by everybody, big or small, made an impact of some degree on the lives of the decision maker, people close to them, and people who played no part in the matter? Well, we do. Imagining that is not required. A careless choice you made a decade ago may have ended up being related to a relevant situation in your hands today. You never know. Just as a butterfly has been quipped to cause a typhoon thousands of miles away from the flapping of its wings, due appreciation for the interconnection of all things is helpful in sorting through personal time lines and even distress. For example, through many other happenstances, if I had not slept through my alarm the Sunday morning on the day of my epiphany, I probably would not have been inspired with another vision, and these missing pieces would most likely not be in your mental possession. It's far from simple to grasp like the metamorphic butterfly appearance from a chrysalis with humble caterpillar beginnings, but we're not supposed to understand everything as human beings. We are simply tasked to trust God in the places we stand today, here and now, and trust what's to come.

Things happen. Of course. We should not become fearful of how jarringly interwoven our experiences can be sometimes. In fact, putting yourself out into the world and giving yourself a real chance is vital to breakthroughs in perspective and the complex web of individual decisions will welcome your contributions, corrupt or correct. So, proceed with caution. Think about your position in life just one year ago. What changed and what changed, drastically? Odds are, you could trace drastic changes back to an origin so miniscule in scope that you'd be taken aback and in disbelief for several minutes. Time gets crazy, and when time seems to speed up, reflection and gratitude for the little things and people fade entirely into darkness. The mind-boggling "butterfly effect" phenomenon should be implemented into thanksgiving thoughts and prayers because of that.

If not much else, this should be meditated on: when you depart from your place of refuge and venture into public spaces, you have an unfathomable amount of possible choices and thus, people with souls and feelings to influence. Picture a profile view of an iceberg. Notice how a massive portion of it is underwater and out of sight from above water level? It's safe to compare that with the awareness, or visibility, of decision effects existing around us. So many of the effects from what we do and say and what we do not do and say are unknown to us. To other people, your actions could have made a profound impact. You never know. Treat the vibrations coming from your mouth with the utmost respect and settle into an ambassadorship for God so you do not have to worry if your complex and vastly interconnected influences are constructed from cheap utterances and misconduct. You and I were not created to add to the list of this world's intentional tortfeasors, so handle opposition from others with grace and abandon the drive to gatekeep your true self from entering the eclectic network. Proceed with caution because again, you simply never know. You could end up being someone's winsome role model and hero without knowing it. Someone's villain, too.

Emulations

Gratefulness is a centerpiece-worthy trait and one that should be held in practice to relieve anguish. If you would, please take a moment to think about the most meaningful people in your life—including the ones who have positively influenced you from the outside without ever having touched you. Do they try to provide you with better things? Do they possess traits that you strive to possess? Do they give you reasons to want to live?

Conceptualize and genuinely appreciate their qualities. Pay homage and make it known to them before we've all faded away.

Here are some examples:

1. [My mother] Theresa
   Her mental fortitude, humor, personability, simplicity, humility, and heroic selflessness. The authentic love and concern she extends to her children and grandchildren. The way she makes volunteering and hospitality appear so effortless. For people to not be boastful and high minded. Of the philosophy that unconditional love and due sacrifice are the keys to successful motherhood. To pray for ill-willed people and uplift those dealing with adversity.

2. [My father] Neil
   His integrity, strong work ethic, warm fellowship, and support. His ability to disregard other people's foolishness and opinions in favor of the truth. The way he will stop on a dime to answer your call and assist loved ones with timeless wisdom. How we can only control what we can control and nothing else. To reminisce with friends and family for hours and provide a glimpse into the tales we've been itching to hear more about. To extend sincere thanks to God for even the most basic daily blessings.

3. [My sister] Stacy
   Her charm, creativity, honest sense of empathy, and strong will. Being slow to anger and quick to share

the warmth of her presence. How she exemplifies the spirit of a joyful one. To express the absolute need for positive energy in our daily lives.

4. [My brother] Scottie
   His long-held compassion, adventurous nature, calmness, humor, and well-mannered communication and courteous habits. How seldom has he been upset or given way to rumors about anybody he has yet to meet. The opposite of a fool. A role model.

5. [My brother] Jason
   His down-to-earth disposition, patience, pragmatic thinking, humor, steadfast intelligence, and compartmentalization skills. The way he captivates others while speaking. How to use every resource you have to its fullest extent always—never wasting away anything. To allow nature to determine the timing of your life's cornerstones.

6. [My brother] Eli
   His ingenuity, genuine spirit, and lighthearted personality. How he always has your back in a pinch and never takes anything too seriously. To have an evident sense of humor and utilize it regularly. To live life to the fullest; unwavering. To be content with what you have while striving to experience more memories.

7. [My brother] Jordan
   His toughness, diligence, practicality, and small-circle mentality. How meticulous his processes are to ensure excellence with his handicraft. To work hard for what you own and play when it's time to play. To preach the necessity of using common sense if nothing else. To make something out of nothing and genuinely connect with individuals you meet along your journey.

8. [My sister] Millie
   Her sound ethics, creativity, and reverence for the ones that paved the way before. How she lights up a room with a smile or quick sarcastic joke. To think outside the box as if there were no box at all. To express yourself purely through art. To not care what others think about you if they simply do not understand.

9. [My sister] Rose
   Her strength, compassion, intelligence, and worry-free mental approach. The way she attributes home to where the heart is. To share your most desirable goods with friends so they can enjoy them, too. To let it be, not paying any mind to minute issues out of our control and respect those who possess opposing philosophies.

Equilibrium

Recall the choice we have between the strain of discipline and the strain of regret. Now that you've picked up and contemplated a fair amount of missing pieces, you can strategically fit your being in a location of potential greatness. How are you to fare in it? Considering you're here, the strain of discipline appears to be written for you, and that is all right, desirable, even. If you wish to achieve your highest potential with your mind closer to actualization, you must be enlightened on the topic of an optimal balance of opposites.

A calm state of mind: equilibrium. The truth is that we've got war and peace, neurosis and stoicism, fear and courage, urgency and relaxation, arrogance and humility, and so many more contrasting forces for our minds to conceptualize. We strive to locate an appropriate blend to maintain steadiness. If you've experienced too much of one or two emotions like fear and anger, for example, it's no wonder why your aura is not at or near equilibrium. Not surprisingly, the root explanation of our compounding issues is simply imbalance(s) in our mind's state. Mind over matter, but, if the matter you consistently held onto is commingled slightly off, you cannot expect results matching those of your highest potential.

By this time, you know that successful relationships with your mind systems involve giving and taking, much like successful, lasting relationships. Giving fear and taking a bit more courage or giving relaxation and taking a healthy amount of obsessive urgency may be required because, for all we know, today may be our final day; ten or eleven breaths from now we could be no more. You should execute those types of barters to recalibrate vital wit. When you're fastened at equilibrium, in your element, and focused solely on the right things, others will need to watch out. You will be dangerous in the right way and as formidable as you could possibly be. Integrating and having a firm understanding of visionary space, feel-good pain, flowing interconnection, and gratitude, equilibrium can have a fighting chance to occur rather quickly. All that remains to be discovered is everything: the wherewithal to know precisely where and who to look to for the clarity and peace facets of your balanced walk through life.

Up

Since you've not only seen but have explored rock bottom without a sliver of hope that you'd recover, you also know faith's appeal all too well. Life is far too complicated for you to memorize every nuance, so you should not even attempt that. Let's leave the master control to God, the power that possesses the ability and desire to spare you from mental wreckage. We are all humans, and we have the same spiritual need—a need encompassing truth in reality, peace, and openness to long suffering and potential persecution despite good intentions. Surrendering yourself and setting aside your pride in favor of a greater cause like thought and prayer for those having a rough go of it. You can spread not only the good news that we can have everlasting life with Jesus Christ upon and instead of death, but also that you've got a real friend in Him forever if you accept what He's sacrificed for you. He is not spiteful toward you for what you've done or for wrongdoing that you've conceptualized. He genuinely wants to see you thrive. Although He may dizzy your world temporarily, His heavenly, eternal plan for you is meaningful and of the utmost relevance for humankind.

If you're at your lowest right now, you may despise yourself. If you're at your lowest right now, your attention may not be focused on the areas that matter, like a divine and omnipotent being. An earnest way you can exercise self-love is to pursue lasting clarity and peace by submitting your heart to the Lord and trusting that He willingly gave His life on the cross and covered the expense of your sin so you can escape from a destiny separated from God and His unimaginably great graces. In addition to all else self-love contributes, with it you will find contentment with your life, and unlike demons, you will not wish to trade just anything for opposing possessions and livelihoods. Claiming that you and I are unworthy of His riches in Heaven is factual, but that does not mean that the ultimate, free gift of salvation should not be accepted. I peacefully encourage you to consider picking up and exploring the Bible alone or with other people, if possible. Let His words speak to you in whichever way they will. The mightiest tangible gift I ever received was a Bible from my father in 2012, and the mightiest spiritual gift I ever received was the Holy Spirit through belief in it. You may find that the more you read the Bible the more the Bible will read you, sparking a mighty self-reinforcing trend of personal and spiritual growth. All it can take is one testament. Your heart has to be softened and your mind open to the reception of His unconditional love and mercy for you along with every other soul.

Imagine if you treated this world like you did as you reflected. Instead of getting out of the body and into your mind, you could get out of this world and into your life and realize that although things are crazy here on earth, there is mental and spiritual renewal to be gained while living. *Memento mori*, though. It cannot be stressed enough that you do not have much more time, but what you could have is true faith in the Lord. It may prove to be easily forgotten, so while you walk nearer to the end times, you should always remember to turn your eyes upon Jesus and His actions for you in days of loss, days of gain, and in days of breaking even. Leave it to Him to guide you. He does not expect you to have all the answers. You and I are children of God, and in a world with darkness seeping in all around, you could accept all that is uncontrollable and shine your bright light. As you break through to access the rest of your existence, do not forget to look up; closer to greatness and the inevitability of it.

Legacy

Well, here you are. The end of the beginning, so to speak. Cheers. Your inevitability of greatness that is tied directly to a vision has seen incredible progress, but there is something you must consider before we depart from this earthly paradise. What comes after this is a total secret. All we know is that the mind relics available have been collected and are in a secure place now. Congratulations. You have achieved mind actualization through the missing pieces to your puzzle. What you were missing, above anything else, was peace. People can steal it from you, so watch over it with dignity, because you and I are not going back. We've got no more moments to spend lost in yesterday.

You've been granted a small section in history to exist within, so *Memento vivere*. It's in your best interest to actually live during your section's phases. What's spectacular is that what you do in your life can influence generations of people upon your passing. The legacy left behind from an actualized mind, not to mention self, is usually far more just than otherwise. The remaining sand in your life-spanning hourglass is not entangled with any sort of game. The actions you take next mean something. They mean more than just something. To consider your life, your legacy, as nothing more than an ongoing joke would be an utter waste given the mathematical probability of even being conceived. And you were positioned fruitfully in a place where life can flourish in our galaxy while having a genuine, blessed chance here.

You were dealt a hand of cards when you entered the chat that is this universe. Was your initial hand good, OK, or downright mediocre? Nevertheless, you must play your hand with a clear mind and be willing to go all in as if your time depends on it. It does. The one and only path to the legacy you wish to leave as a parting gift is disciplined, unrelenting, passionate work. It's possible to experience unreal feelings simply by being real and spreading clean, virtuous energy into the world. Remain true to yourself, your mental visions, and what you stand for, and you'll be in disbelief at the impact you made when it's all said and done and you've lived your legacy.

Printed in the United States
by Baker & Taylor Publisher Services